HORN OF SAMUEL

Heaven's Trumpet Call of Liberty
To Those Hurt by Abortion.

Jim,

May the message of this stanza of "Amazing Grace" touch many hearts and souls — and set them all free — throughout the land!

Reed Allen

Heaven's Trumpet Call of Liberty

HORN OF SAMUEL

Heaven's Trumpet Call of Liberty To Those Hurt by Abortion.

Copyright © 2010 by David Allen

All rights reserved in all countries. No part of this material may be reproduced, stored in a retrieval system, or transmitted in any form or by any means electronic, mechanical, photocopying, recording, or otherwise without prior written permission of the author, publisher and/or copyright owners, except as provided by USA copyright law.

Published and Printed By Dare 2 Dream Books
Pearland, TX (405) 642-8257

Cover by Tremaine Fowler, MyGospelVoice.com
Houston, TX (832) 818-3327

Publisher's Cataloging in Publication

Allen David: Horn of Samuel
    1. Counseling 2. Psychology 3. Christianity 4. Discipleship

978-0-9779694-1-8

Horn of Samuel

FORWARD

"PROCLAIM LIBERTY THROUGHOUT ALL THE LAND UNTO ALL THE INHABITANTS THEREOF"
Leviticus 25:10
Cast in bronze on the Liberty Bell

There were only two weeks to prepare for the trial against Planned Parenthood. During that time, I received some new lyrics for the old hymn, "Amazing Grace."

They spoke of the mommies and daddies hurt by abortion. I cried as I remembered my own son, Samuel, and heard the "trumpet call" of Liberty:

Amazing grace, how sweet the sound,
That comes from round your throne.
The sound of the babes, singing mercy and grace,
For mommies and daddies to come home.

Their chains are gone, they've been set free,
My God, My Savior, has ransomed them.
And like a flood, His mercy reigns,
Unending love, amazing grace.

Glory, Glory, Alleluia,
His mercy is coming, like a flood.

by Pastor Tim Nothaker, Living Waters Ministry

Heaven's Trumpet Call of Liberty

Court Transcripts

Three different Court Reporters played an essential role in transcribing the Court proceedings for this book. Appreciation is extended to Clarisia, Phyllis, and Walter whose efforts were essential in accurately recording the courtroom proceedings.

Horn of Samuel

DEDICATION

This "Trumpet Call" is for all the mommies and daddies, grandmas and grandpas, and everyone else hurt by abortion. Many of you—especially you moms and dads—share with me the unspeakable grief of not being able to know and hold our lost children.

But now, hear the trumpet call, "It is <u>not</u> over! You are still to share in God's love for your children, just the way He always intended. It is <u>not</u> over."

Your children are safe in His arms. This trumpet call is for you. And, it sounds the Liberty that God has already provided for you. This Liberty allows you to know and love your children.

The deceit of abortion first lures us in, and then uses our broken hearts to imprison and silence us. While our babies surround God's throne, we remain imprisoned and forbidden to grieve.

The Bible says that no mistake you could ever make is bigger than God's love for you. And with that infinite love, the chains of guilt and shame are broken. The prison doors are opened wide.

The deceptive tyranny of abortion flees before the light of God's love—the same love demonstrated upon a cross on a hill called Calvary. There, God gave His own Child to a bloody death for you and for me. He did it knowing that we were yet sinners (Romans 5:8).

And His love for _____ [*your name here*] was proven, once and for all, when Jesus rose again, and a victorious trumpet announced, "Our God Reigns!"

By His great love, you are restored. By repenting and giving your broken heart to God, you receive Liberty to love Him and to love your children.

It is time to give our children names. It is time to love them and hold them in a kingdom where there are no tears.

Be assured, that no matter what, you are a precious child to your Father God. He has called you and is waiting for your response. Simply say:

"Father God, help me to know Your love. I believe Your Son, Jesus, died on the cross at Calvary for my sins, and rose again. I surrender all my sins to You. Please heal my broken heart and fill it with the Love of heaven."

TABLE OF CONTENTS

1.	The Trumpet Call	1
2.	Getting Involved	4
3.	The Arraignment	9
4.	The Prosecutor Requests a Jury	16
5.	The Prosecutor Requests a Deal	22
6.	My Son is Named Samuel	26
7.	Arriving at Court	33
8.	First Attempt to Take My Jesus	35
9.	Second Attempt to Take My Jesus	42
10.	The Prosecution Motions to Limit the Defense	49
11.	Jury Selection	52
12.	The Prosecution Begins	55
13.	The Purple Shirt	64
14.	The Video	71
15.	An Early Morning Walk	76
16.	The Defense Begins	81
17.	Qualification and Ownership	90
19.	The Trumpet Sounds in the Court	100
20.	Cross Examination	104
21.	Redirect	110
22.	Final Arguments	120
23.	The Verdict	141
24.	The Lion of Judah	145
	PS The Proof	151
	PPS A Final Blessing	156

Heaven's Trumpet Call of Liberty

This former Sterling Bank building is now Houston's new Planned Parenthood Headquarters—and the largest abortion clinic in America.

CHAPTER 1
THE TRUMPET CALL

On March 18, 2010, I walked around the outside of a seven story building that was being remodeled into the largest abortion clinic in America. Located on the Gulf Freeway in Houston, Texas, it is just south of the heart of the city. Landscapers, electricians, painters, and other tradesmen, were hurrying to meet a completion deadline less than two months away.

Planned Parenthood, the "Giant" of the abortion industry, was behind the project. This was to be a flagship headquarters, complete with a third floor surgical suite specially designed and equipped to perform late term abortions.

The project was located in the midst of four poor neighborhoods and adjacent the University of Houston, both traditional targets of the abortion industry.

From the personal experience shared in Chapter 6, I knew the term "Parenthood" was deceptive—its mission is not parenthood.

I'd known the hurt of its deception. But now, I was no longer a frightened young man. I was a seasoned Christian, trained to carry the gospel of heaven's Love into dark and fearful places.

On the sidewalk was another group—their heads lowered in quiet prayer. They were pleading for the lives the building was being prepared to take.

At each corner of the fence, I stopped to sound the 'shofar'.

The shofar, or "rams horn," is the trumpet that was used to bring down the walls of Jericho (Joshua 6:4). A Jewish tradition, the shofar has spread in recent years to Christian communities around the world. I'd studied and learned the skill and was often called to sound at churches and events in and around the city.

I visited this building almost daily, usually on my lunch hour. I found that the 'trumpet call' encouraged those praying. Like the story of Jericho, they would sometimes shout joyfully as the shofar sounded.

Until this day, it had never occurred to me to sound inside the building, but as I awoke that morning, I had the thought, "Blow the trumpet in the heart of the "Giant." The thought would not relent and by lunchtime, I was still wrestling with it.

I usually sounded from the sidewalk or street, but as a compromise with the persistent thought, I set out to sound the outside corners of the wrought iron fence that surrounded the building.

Horn of Samuel

As I sounded the fourth corner, a construction superintendent yelled at me from inside the fence, "You're on private property! You're gonna get arrested!"

At that instant, I knew I was going into the building. I called back, "God bless you," and walked around toward the front gate.

On the sidewalk I paused to greet some ladies who were praying. They pleaded with me not to go in and warned me for the second time, "You'll be arrested."

Oddly, with each warning, came an inner peace and confidence as I thought, "How dare this deceitful giant trespass in my city."

I assured them, "Don't worry. I'm going in, and I'm coming out." A complete sense of protection had come over me.

I strode through the open parking lot gate, past an angry security guard, through the open double doors, and into the lobby. After pausing to warn about twenty workmen that I was going to "sound this horn," I closed my eyes and slowly raised the shofar to my lips. Several shofar calls reverberated throughout all seven floors of the building.

After the moment of silence that followed, I announced to the workmen, "I know you're just here earning a living, but you just have to know—you are loved! You are precious to your Father God!"

And then I left.

CHAPTER 2
GETTING INVOLVED

I was first drawn to the "Pro-Life" movement in the early months of 2010, and experienced the growing "tension" around the issue of abortion. Word had spread that people were coming from all over the United States to Houston to pray and actively demonstrate for an end to abortion in America.

There would be a large gathering at Grace Community Church, a few miles further south on the Gulf Freeway. The next day there would be a rally and a march to the site of Parenthood's renovation project.

In January of 2010, on my way to the church, I would have to pass by the project site. I planned to stop and sound the shofar.

As I arrived and prepared to sound, I was disappointed to find myself alone. Closing my eyes, I prayed to be part of an army. Opening my eyes moments later, I saw a group of seven strangers approaching.

One of them was Mary, a passionate "Pro-Life" worker from Houston. In the months to come she would be a constant source of encouragement as events unfolded. She tenderly cradled a ceramic baby in her arms as if it were alive. The rest of the group were from Arkansas and

Oklahoma and had come to march around the building, Jericho style, before attending the gathering.

We greeted each other and rejoiced as I sounded the shofar and they shouted. The cacophony washed over the building, and we prayed and thanked God that the dark, spiritual walls of abortion were coming down.

Arriving later at the church, I met John, another shofar sounder. Together we sounded the four corners of the church property to "prepare the way" for the service.

That evening the thousands who had come prayed earnestly, repenting and pleading with God to end abortion in America (2 Chronicles 7:14). They also praised and worshipped God in joyful anticipation of a victory that simply must be—and that must be His.

In the months that followed, I would sound the shofar at the remodeling project, and Parenthood's old, one story headquarters clinic on Fannin Street. It had been the scene of over 300,000 abortions.

At both locations, "Pro-Life" workers sought to share the message of God's love and mercy. A faithful cadre of sidewalk counselors and prayer intercessors was slowly growing, armed with the most powerful of weapons—God's love. Many shared testimonies of babies lost to abortion.

Mary was there often, cradling her precious baby and fearlessly loving and counseling those coming and going. She loved to sing, and the iron fence was powerless to stop the sweet melodies of Jesus' love from wafting into the buildings. I came to know many of the "Pro-Life" workers, and we all found great joy standing together in this cause. The occasional miracle story of a mother or a couple electing to have their babies kept us all going strong.

It was on these sidewalks that I first publicly and tearfully shared my own testimony of the abortion of my son Samuel. Later, a counselor would share my story with a young man who was waiting outside for his girlfriend to have an abortion. Hearing of Samuel and my regrets, he went in and brought her out. They were both joyful and relieved. He waved the $900 cash that he'd brought to pay for the abortion and said, "They'll never get this!" When I heard this, I knew that one child was alive because of Samuel, and that I would never leave this battle.

At my age, I could remember the Civil Rights movement of the 1960's, and the "tension" that existed around segregation. The nightly news brought vivid footage of police attacking those who would dare gather to march in prayer and sing about freedom.

There was a "trumpet call" of heaven's love then, as television cameras exposed the tyranny of segregation that forced the authorities to uphold dehumanizing laws with dogs, water cannons and tear gas.

Horn of Samuel

The "tension" grew until that trumpet call reached the heart of the nation. We could no longer tolerate segregation. The laws and regulations that protected it fell away. God's Liberty was declared to all the inhabitants of the land—on all sides of the issue. The God-given rights to life and liberty were restored.

Today, the dehumanizing laws that protect abortion are also shaking. But, this time television is largely controlled by the same deceptive forces that promote abortion. Its transmissions offend God's design by conferring upon men the role of judging who will live and who will die. But whenever given such power over others, men have proven to be merciless judges.

****

But, what about the victims of abortion that are left behind? There are now so many of us, and the emotional wounds are so well documented, that the abortion industry can no longer deny them. Yet, that industry can't promote the needed healing process because that would expose the deception that a "fetus is not a child."

So the deception must cause society to ignore the wounds. No funerals. No obituaries. No caskets. No headstones. No hugs or condolences. The tiny bodies heartlessly disposed of with the garbage.

Those left behind to grieve are then silenced by the same deception that first told them their children were not human. It now forbids them from mourning.

The deceit is complete as grieving moms and dads are abandoned to an inner prison of guilt and regret. In their hearts they miss the God-given blessings that they'd been told were "liabilities." They long to know their children and hold them—the way God designed.

But, the deception of abortion requires they remain silent. It cannot allow the trumpet sound of God's love to reach the captives the way it did in the 1960's. These captives must not be allowed to know of God's Liberty—of His love and His forgiveness.

What would happen if the growing number of grieving parents and other family members, now over 150 million adults in the U.S. alone, heard that trumpet call?

Why...All heaven would break loose.

CHAPTER 3
THE ARRAIGNMENT

Meanwhile, my vehicle license number was being traced by the Houston Police Department. Six days after sounding the shofar inside Parenthood's new flagship clinic, I received a call from Officer [Kenneth].

As I answered his questions over the phone, he was understanding and considerate. But, he advised that Parenthood might choose to press charges. If that happened, he said I'd have to come downtown and be "booked." Kenneth would call back several times in the coming days with updates as the charges worked their way through channels for signature.

About a week after Kenneth's initial call, I woke up early and felt led to go downtown and sound the shofar before work. I arrived before dawn and sounded from the steps of City Hall. The soulful calls reverberated back from the surrounding skyscrapers.

Something then seemed to say, "Sound at the Wells Fargo Plaza." It was only a block away, and as I sounded outward from the front sidewalk there, I heard the doorman calling and running toward me.

Slowly lowering the shofar, I turned to see what kind of trouble I was in. But he greeted me with a big smile, and excitedly recalled that he'd seen me sounding at the intersection of "Fannin and San Jacinto Streets" and that we'd spoken then.

After exchanging words of encouragement, he returned to his duties. I would not appreciate this encounter until later in the day.

In the office later that morning, I received a call from Officer [Kenneth]. He was apologetic as he explained that charges had been signed and I would need to come downtown and post a $500 bond.

At a crowded Harris County Sheriff's building, I joined a line of people being processed, photographed, and fingerprinted. I was saddened to see some singled out, handcuffed, and taken through a passageway to the adjacent county jail.

As my "booking" was completed, an arraignment date was set for April 13th. I left the crowded building feeling relieved that I'd not been taken down the passageway, but saddened by the de-humanizing process. It seemed strange to be accused for sounding God's love against something these very authorities should be stopping.

As I pulled away from the curb, the first stop was at a T-intersection. There, I looked up to see a street sign directly in front of me. It had two arrows, pointing in opposite directions. One pointed to "Fannin Street" and the other to "San Jacinto Street!" The same two streets the doorman had mentioned that morning.

I didn't remember the past encounter with the doorman, or even sounding there, but obviously I'd sounded a preparatory trumpet call on this very corner. I began singing a hymn as a renewed spirit of confidence filled me. I remembered that there was a "heavenly Defender" protecting me.

****

On April 13th, driving downtown to the arraignment, I debated whether to wear my Tallit into the courtroom.

The Tallit, or "prayer shawl" has tassels on each corner representing God's Word. It honors the Biblical direction to hang God's Word from the four corners one's garments (Numbers 15:38-39). They are to remind us of the protective, healing covering of the Word of God. To Christians, this "Word" is literally, Jesus (John 1:1). I wanted my heavenly Defender, Jesus, to be covering me.

I felt a cheerful confidence as I parked and donned the Tallit. In the brisk morning air, I walked the short distance to the Harris County Criminal Court building. I brought my shofar because in the event of a trial, I wanted to know the procedure for getting it through security.

On the sidewalk in front of the court building was Ricky, a street vendor who encouraged judges, policemen, prosecutors and defendants alike with the dual messages of "God Bless You!" and "You are loved!" They accompanied his sales pitch for M&M's and umbrellas. We'd gotten acquainted on my preliminary visits to the courthouse, and he always called out, "Blow tha' horn! Blow tha' horn!" And I always obliged.

This morning was no different, and as I finished sounding, I was again encouraged to see in front of the courthouse, another shofar brother, Willie, and his wife, there to pray, sound the shofar, and stand with me. There were also some "Pro-Life" friends, praying on the sidewalk with their well-worn signs. It was encouraging to see every one of them, and to know I was not alone.

At the security check point, they took my shofar and issued a claim check in exchange. I took the crowded elevator to the 11th floor, and entered Courtroom 14.

There, Defendants and lawyers all waited to address various matters before the Court. As each case was processed, the Defendant would stand before the Judge's bench. The Judge would listen and ask questions, and then provide a ruling or other guidance.

There was something special about this Judge. He spoke with empathy and the gentle authority of a father counseling his children. I'd come to hold him in the highest esteem.

Horn of Samuel

Judge [Michael] is a family man whose wife of many years serves on the Houston Police Department. After his years in the Army and attending law school, he'd worked in the District Attorney and the Texas Attorney General Offices. Judge [Michael] was first elected to his bench in 1998, and had long established a reputation for fairness and integrity. He was also an ordained minister and active in his church. He also found time to serve in the community, and with troubled youth organizations.

It was late in the morning when my case was called. As I took my place before the bench, a young Prosecutor smirked as he announced, "And now... for the Trumpeter!" He then read the charges involving a "Class B Misdemeanor Trespass."

The events he described were familiar, but I was surprised to hear him allege that I had pushed the security guard. That was not true, and I thought, "If that were so, why am I not charged with assault?"

The false allegation instantly clarified how I would plead. From that moment, I knew a "Guilty" plea or any "plea bargain" with Parenthood or those representing it would be bowing to its deceit.

When the Judge asked for my plea, I said, "Not Guilty."

The Judge then advised that I had the right to have a trial heard before a Jury, or I could waive that right and have it heard before him.

I chose to waive a Jury trial, and agreed that he would hear the case. The trial date was set for April 29—just two weeks later.

The Judge went on to stress my right to an attorney and that one could be appointed if I was indigent. I stated that I was not indigent, and would appear Pro-Se, meaning "representing oneself". I sensed strongly that my heavenly Defender was sufficient.

The Judge advised that this was my right, but asked that I speak with Mr. [Dan], a public defender working in his courtroom that day.

I'd noticed Dan assisting other Defendants, and agreed to speak with him. Outside the Courtroom we spoke briefly, but he had to finish some business before we could meet. When he directed me to wait in a small conference room, I expressed a preference to wait in the open hallway. He became incensed, and angrily pointed to the small room, ordering me to sit there until he was available. Startled, I instinctively replied, "Yes sir."

However, after he left, I prayed and departed. I called the Court later to express my appreciation for the Judge's concern, but that I didn't think Dan would be the best adviser in this particular case.

I would later speak with a number of "Pro-Life" and other attorneys offering to assist. However, they all seemed focused on some kind of compromise to get me "off the hook." None of them appreciated that my Defender and I were about to face a deceitful giant together.

CHAPTER 4
THE PROSECUTOR REQUESTS A JURY

One week before the trial, on the morning of April 22nd, I was working in my office when the phone rang. My wife was calling to say the Court had just called the house, wanting to speak with me.

Promising to call her back as soon as I knew what it was about, I called the Court, and was put on hold. Moments later, the Judge came on the line, and we exchanged greetings.

He said the call would have to be on the record with the Court Reporter transcribing. He asked if that would be Okay, and I agreed. Once on the record, he advised that the State of Texas was exercising its right to request a Jury trial. Making the request to the Court was the District Attorney Division Head, Ms. [Kate].

The Judge explained that, while I'd agreed to have him hear the case, the State also had the right to request a Jury trial. He then reiterated my right to counsel, and asked if I still wanted to waive the right to an attorney.

I had a sense of peace, and understood why the Prosecutor needed this Class B Misdemeanor Trespass case heard by a Jury. They were not comfortable with this Judge. He was a conservative family man and an ordained minister. Parenthood would be demanding that they deliver a "Guilty" verdict for this affront to its new flagship clinic.

It would also be critical because both the previous mayor, Bill White, and the current mayor, Anise Parker, were Parenthood supporters. They'd welcomed the new mega-facility to Houston. Mayor Parker would be the honored speaker and cut the ribbon at the opening ceremony scheduled in just a few weeks. Bill White had graduated to become a "Pro-Choice" candidate for Governor.

Anything but a conviction would be unacceptable. Toward this end, the District Attorney's Office devoted a four-person team of prosecuting attorneys, with support staff, to prosecute this misdemeanor case. They would prepare 28 prosecution exhibits, including maps, photographs, CD's, and videos. In addition, roughly a dozen District Attorneys would attend just to observe the trial.

How many innocents would the giant take while these District Attorney resources were spent prosecuting this "offender?"

Under the deception of abortion, and the court rulings it has manipulated into being, District Attorneys are required to ignore the violence of abortion and to serve the "Giant" that violates the divine laws of God's Love.

In this case, Parenthood had to press charges and silence this offensive "trumpet call" that was such a highly visible affront to its agenda. How dare the trumpet call of God's Liberty be sounded in the very heart of their grandest clinic ever!

The Prosecutors would also need to cover for the city leaders who had allied with the deception. They must prevail against this brazen challenge to these leaders' applause and official ceremonies that had welcomed this "Giant" into the heart of the city. The city they'd been elected to serve and protect.

I cheerfully agreed to a Jury trial and assured the Judge that I was looking forward to having the case heard on April 29th, as scheduled. He then reiterated the importance of having an attorney.

I expressed my desire to do the right thing and not to embarrass the Court. He assured me that I was not going to do that and said he would have had someone sit "second chair" in any case. I asked the meaning of that term, and he explained that I would retain control of the case, but an attorney would be there to assist with protocol. I expressed my appreciation for his concern and said I would be willing.

The Judge also advised that if there were an attorney appointed, the rules allowed an extension to prepare for trial. He encouraged me to use this time. However, I had a strong sense that the original date had been set for a reason.

By the end of the trial, it would become clear why this date was important.

During my preparation for trial, between the demands of my regular job and the responsibilities of raising three boys, ages 9 to 12, there was little time to prepare. Throughout this time, my wife, with deep concern for our family, prayed faithfully.

The maximum penalty was a $2,000 fine and 180 days in jail. The fine would not be a problem, but I didn't have that much vacation time.

I also received invaluable assistance from a friend I'd met in the "Pro-Life" movement. Steven had attended law school, and provided much helpful information on courtroom procedures and precedents.

Steven was also a gentle and tireless leader, devoted to sidewalk counseling of people on both sides of the issue, and to providing leadership and encouragement to countless "Pro-Life" workers.

Even the staff and security of Parenthood appreciated his sincere heart and would find occasion to confide in him privately, sharing their own questions and heartaches, and receiving his understanding and solace.

Steven's passions included filming and producing "Pro-Life" videos under the name, "Spiritus Films." He'd recently interviewed Abby Johnson, a former Parenthood director, and national employee of the year. Abby had to witness an "ultrasound abortion," and was shocked to see a baby struggling hopelessly against the abortion instruments intruding into its womb. She came to realize that unborn babies are just as alive and human as her own small children.

Abby left Parenthood to become a leading spokesperson for life. Steven's video interview revealed the joy Abby experienced once freed from the dark bonds of the abortion industry.

Sensing the need to record a video of what was happening in my case, Steven had me meet him several days before the trial to film an interview. I chose the steps of City Hall as the location. City Hall had also been the setting for many shofar gatherings in recent years and represented the heart of the city.

That interview can be viewed by an on line search of "Horn of Samuel," or links http://blip.tv/file/3578988, or http://spiritusfilms.com.

I was scheduled to sound the shofar on these same steps at a praise and worship rally a few weeks after the

Horn of Samuel

trial—that trumpet call would be amplified by enormous speakers and would blast the reverberating "sound of heaven" all through the center of the city.

Two other shofar brothers, Willie and Lloyd, joined us for the interview along with family and friends. Steven was used to asking questions to guide his interviews, but after one question, my words just flowed as I released my feelings in those rushed days.

During the interview, Lloyd felt led to sound his shofar at certain times, and it is these calls, unedited and divinely timed, that are heard during the interview.

This video testifies that the darkness of abortion is fleeing from the Love of heaven. God's laws of life and liberty cannot be denied by the laws of men forever. When governments and courts offend God's laws, there is always "tension" until God's laws prevail.

Three weeks after the trial, David Allen sounds the shofar on the steps of City Hall to open a Praise and Worship gathering. Large speakers reverberated the sound powerfully into the surrounding skyscrapers.

CHAPTER 5
THE PROSECUTOR REQUESTS A DEAL

After they requested a Jury trial that morning, I was surprised when two District Attorneys called me at home that same evening to offer a settlement "deal." Ms. [Stacey] and her supervisor Ms. [Rachel] explained that they had been directed by Ms. [Kate], their Division Head, to offer a Pre-Trial Diversion.

I first thanked them for the job they do to protect our city and our families. They then presented an offer that would require my signing an agreement limiting my activities at Parenthood's facilities.

I thanked them for the offer and agreed to consider it. Towards the end of the conversation, I used the opportunity to ask about the Prosecutor's accusation during the arraignment, that I'd pushed a security guard. This seemed to make them uncomfortable, but I pressed on and asked that, if this were the case, why assault charges were not being filed?

They talked around my question without answering. I persisted, and eventually they assured me that no such charge was being considered. I pressed further, and got them to agree that this accusation would not be raised during trial.

The District Attorney's confusion in requesting a Jury trial in the morning, and offering a deal that evening, reflected a turmoil I would see throughout the trial. In their hearts, they did not want to represent this unsavory "Giant," but Parenthood and its political allies would demand that they do so. And do so well.

This confusion was apparent again the next morning—this time before the Judge. I had to drop by the courtroom to pick up some original documents. When the Judge noticed me in the courtroom, he asked that I approach the bench.

As we greeted each other he seemed pleased and said he was glad to hear that the State had contacted me about a settlement offer.

As I began to confirm his understanding, we were both startled by a loud voice interrupting from my right. Standing next to me, the DA Division Head, Ms. [Kate], asserted firmly that this was not the case, and that the State had no intention of making any such an offer. She added that the prosecution fully intended to proceed to trial. The Judge and I exchanged surprised looks as she handed me the documents I'd come for.

The confusion continued as District Attorneys [Stacey] and [Rachel] would call several more times to pressure me into accepting their offer. Each time I would thank them for their efforts, but I had a peace all along, knowing that I wanted nothing to do with any agreement involving "Parenthood."

On April 27th, two days before the trial, the Prosecutors called for the last time about their offer. They followed up the call with an e-mail that included a link to a YouTube video.

Parenthood's Head of Security, Ms. [Larissa] had recorded me preaching a brief message at the Fannin clinic, and sounding the shofar. The Prosecutors inferred that they would use this video against me if I did not agree to their deal.

I smiled. I'd already been told about the video, which could be viewed by searching on-line for "Shofar Guy", and was pleased to see it on line. On several occasions, seeing Larissa's camera, I'd use the opportunities to preach about God's Love. I knew this particular message was one of Freedom.

I knew it would demonstrate to the Jury, the message of God's Love that I'd always shared on Parenthood's sidewalks. Coincidentally, on several visits to the courthouse prior to the trial, I'd heard Ricky, a sidewalk vendor, joyfully sharing the same message, "You Are Loved."

The video the District Attorneys thought I'd fear, was a "present with a bow." I smiled as I transcribed the words from the video for use at the trial.

The words reflected exactly what I'd expressed with the shofar in the lobby of the new building,

"Freedom Lord to live. Freedom Lord to love. Freedom to walk in the light of Your purpose. Thy Kingdom come, Thy Will be done this day Lord. In Your precious name we pray, Jesus our Savior."

I believed that no Jury could convict me for bringing this message of freedom and love into a place being constructed for just the opposite purpose.

CHAPTER 6
MY SON IS NAMED SAMUEL

My involvement with Parenthood had actually begun in the early 1970's. This chapter explains how and why I was uniquely qualified to sound the trumpet call in Parenthood's new flagship clinic.

Growing up in the idyllic coastal community of Coronado, California, I selfishly thought the white sand beaches and endless days of surfing and sailing existed just for me. I was the center of the universe and could just reach out and take whatever I pleased.

In the summer of 1971, before my senior year of high school, I met a delightful girl with a bright smile and a happy heart. Her family had just moved in down the street, and she would be a sophomore at my school. She loved the beach as much as I did, and we surfed and sailed through the summer together. We became fast friends and then high school sweethearts.

She'd grown up in a loving home, and her parents welcomed me into their family. She loved art classes, and her beautiful projects were always presents for me. She completely trusted me with her heart.

Horn of Samuel

But in 1973, shortly after I'd graduated, she became pregnant. Despite our relationship, my only concern was how this would affect my own dreams.

As we faced this pregnancy, I did not see a precious new baby and a lovely young mother, but rather the need to avoid the consequences of my actions.

It so happened that the U.S. Supreme Court had issued a ruling just months earlier, in a case called "Roe v. Wade." It was breathtaking in its scope, overthrowing the protective laws of 50 states, and conferring to American citizens, broad rights to decide which unborn children would live, and which would not.

We'd heard about the case, and flowed with the tide of popular opinion supporting it at the time. We could not imagine the heartache it would bring us.

Just as Parenthood planned, we were ushered into a storefront office, and found a straightforward solution to our "problem."

She was 16 at the time, and there was apparently no requirement to inform her parents. In secret, we drove to Children's Hospital in San Diego.

After being examined, she was left on a gurney, exposed to passersby. When she asked to be covered, she was humiliated by a nurse who told her coldly, "You should have thought of that before." After it was over, another nurse told her, "It was a boy."

A dark sadness filled the car on the drive home, as she shared these deep hurts with me. We left the tiny remains of our firstborn child behind.

Our relationship withered, along with her bright smile. Abortion is a hidden sadness. It cannot be shared and it is not "appropriate" to grieve. Its consequences manifest in lowered self esteem, as once high ideals are crumpled by addictions, depression, and other devastating consequences.

It became my darkest secret, and I know it was hers as well. As we went our separate ways, serious problems would follow each of us—the bad fruit that abortion produces.

I expected the sadness to fade away, but instead it was a nagging heartache that grew slowly stronger, like a choking vine. It was not my only secret; but it was by far the darkest.

I'd kept this secret through two failed marriages. I divorced my first wife in 1980, for purely selfish reasons, and hurt her and her family deeply.

A second marriage would be unhappy, except for two beautiful sons who'd arrived in 1985 and 1989. My second wife left me in 1989, taking our two little boys, and in a divorce I did not want, I tasted the hurt I'd caused my first wife.

Through all this, no matter the rationale justifying abortion, I knew in my heart, that I'd taken the life of my first son, and had then hurt many other people with my selfishness. Now, all this seemed to be surfacing at once to accuse me. And a long-suppressed grief process for my first son was finally beginning.

Growing up, I'd learned the 10 commandments as God's rules. Almost twenty years later, as I turned 38, I realized I'd broken them all.

After my boys were taken from me, I moved East to be near them, but was then transferred to a project in Louisiana. And there, for the first time in my life, I was fired.

That evening, I sat alone on a grassy slope, looking out over the Mississippi River. I sensed a journey was beginning that I could not control. And there I felt the urgent need to read my Bible.

I'd had similar feelings before, but each time I'd tried, I'd be convicted by the passage I chose to read and would close the Bible to go my own way.

But now, something made me search through my trunk and pull it out. I began reading with a passion—an insatiable hunger for the New Testament that this time, would continue unabated. I wanted to learn everything I could about Jesus and what He had said.

While confident that I would soon be re-employed, no companies were interested in talking to me. I loaded my pickup truck with all I had left, and began a physical and spiritual journey westward. Staying with a series of friends and relatives, I progressed along a road that stretched from Louisiana to the Pacific coast.

The journey lasted all summer, as things grew more and more desperate. My savings were quickly gone, and my numerous debts seemed overwhelming. My pride was crumbling into humility.

After almost 5 months, I was staying with an Aunt in the San Francisco area. Buried in debt, and no longer able to visit my two boys, I would occasionally lie on the carpet and weep. There was a vivid sense of falling into a black pit with nothing to hold on to.

Each morning, I would make calls and send out resumes, but by now I expected nothing but silence or rejection. In the afternoons, I would escape for long walks. As each past wrong or debt would come to mind, I'd say, "Let it go, trust in God." The reminders were so relentless that I would say over and over, "Let it go, trust in God... Let it go, trust in God...Let it go, trust in God..."

I continued to read my Bible hungrily—only there could I find peace. I was getting to know and trust Jesus.

And then, on August 17, 1992, a miracle happened. I was walking along a cool, shaded trail in a redwood forest above Oakland. I'd gone there to be alone with God. Leaving the trail, I found a secluded spot and sat down on the soft forest floor. I looked up at the treetops waving against a blue afternoon sky. And in complete silence, I entered my "Guilty" plea before God.

"Father God, I see now how I've taken a life and hurt so many people. I'm destitute—but that's fine—I don't care. And I'm homeless—and that's Okay—it doesn't matter. But, there is just one thing I must ask. Lord Jesus, if You would, please take this mess I've made of my life. It's too heavy for me. I can't carry it anymore."

There was a sense of peace walking back to the parking lot. Typing a letter the next morning, the phone rang. It was my old company telling me they wanted me back in Pennsylvania right away. I loaded up the pickup and began the cross country drive, sleeping in a pup tent.

During the trip, I had a second offer from a company which needed me on a project in Boston right away. After a stop at my old company in Pennsylvania, I went on to see my boys in Virginia, and while we were at a water park playing, I received a third offer. The first offer had come less than 24 hours after my prayer—and three in less than a week! And that after no one would even talk with me for 5 months.

I took the job in Boston and began the process of paying off all my debts. I found a Bible-based church, where I came to understand I'd been "saved" and where I would be baptized. There I met a beautiful Christian lady named Anna, who accepted me even after I told her all my secrets. She seemed to genuinely love my two boys that came up for regular visits.

Anna insisted on a proper courtship, which seemed much too long for me, but she would eventually agree to marry me. We have been blessed with three wonderful boys of our own, and a beautiful home. My two older sons are on their own, both wonderful success stories.

But early in our courtship, I knew it was important to share with Anna, my abortion secret. In response, she offered her forgiveness, and reminded me of God's.

During this process, I felt led to give my first son, whom I had aborted, a name. I named him Samuel. I now knew that God had knitted Samuel in his mother's womb, and would always love and care for him.

While Samuel is lost to us in this present time, he lives with his true Father, and they have both forgiven me, and are waiting to welcome me into a kingdom where there can only be forgiveness and love, and where there are no tears.

CHAPTER 7
ARRIVING AT COURT

In the two weeks since the arraignment, I'd been busy with work and family, but had managed to read over the legal advice I'd received, scribble some outline notes, and prepare a few exhibits.

A friend, Peggy, had told me to gather and carry five stones, like the shepherd boy David, when he faced the giant, Goliath. These were in my pocket, and I felt David's confidence—the Parenthood giant was coming down.

Arriving downtown early, I parked in a public garage. I'd wanted some time before Court to walk and sound the shofar among the tall buildings. I prayed and donned my Tallit, and went out—covered by my heavenly Defender and armed with a notepad and a shofar.

After only a few blocks, my cell phone rang. I stood in a vacant lot and listened as a friend prayed, declaring that no weapon formed against me would prosper.

As we said good-bye, I looked up to see someone waving from across the street. As I approached, I saw that it was Mary. Coincidentally, she had just parked in a city lot across from where I'd been standing.

This chance meeting was blocks from the Courthouse, and even more remarkable because she had something important to share before the trial.

From her daily devotional, she read the message for that day, April 29th. It was about Corrie Ten Boom, a survivor of horrible abuse in World War II concentration camps. Later in her life, Corrie had been called to minister forgiveness and love to her former tormenters. The quote from Corrie Ten Boom's own words:

"I once spoke to a group of prisoners about the passage, "You are the light of the world." I showed them that after they received the Lord Jesus as their Savior, they had the duty of being the light in the darkness of that prison.

One of the men said, "Fellows, this morning I read in the Bible about three murderers. Their names were Moses, David, and Paul. We know them as heroes of God, but all three were murderers. Look what God did with this trio of murderers! There is hope for you—and for me!"

I wept, knowing what I'd done to my son Samuel. And yet, I knew I'd been forgiven. What's more, I'd been given the honor of testifying today of my love for Samuel. I would stand against the same "Giant" I'd given him to.

The encouragement of Mary's message was heaven sent. After we'd prayed and parted, I continued my walk among the tall buildings. With renewed confidence, I sounded the trumpet call of God's Liberty.

CHAPTER 8
FIRST ATTEMPT TO TAKE MY JESUS

Checking my shofar at the security checkpoint, I took a crowded elevator to the 11th floor and entered Criminal Courtroom No. 14. The gallery pews at the rear were crowded with Defendants and their lawyers, as well as pro—life supporters and some fellow shofar sounders.

There was only one seat left—a folding chair placed sideways, directly toward the prosecutor's table a few feet away. From my close-up profile vantage, I could see the Prosecutor was in his early 40's, handsome and well dressed. He had an air of confidence, and I sensed that we'd be friends in any other setting.

Joshua was a successful attorney with the Harris County District Attorney's Office, specializing in helping the victims of domestic violence. He and his wife of over 20 years, had met as freshmen attending Houston's Rice University. Both avid Rice supporters, they held season ticket to the Rice Owls baseball and basketball teams.

Joshua's wife was a beloved OB-Gyn doctor who had delivered thousands of babies for the city of

Heaven's Trumpet Call of Liberty

Houston. They had two handsome teenagers of their own. I learned later that Joshua's devotion to his wife included an ongoing, impassioned search for a compatible stem cell donor to treat a bone marrow disease his wife had been diagnosed with.

At the defense table was an elderly Public Defender with a full white beard, balding head, and wearing an ancient brown Corduroy jacket. He reminded me of the Bible's suffering prophet, Jeremiah.

As I watched, the elderly gentleman came over to the prosecutor's table, and bent over to confer with Joshua. I could not avoid their exchange from my close-up view of their profiles.

Suddenly, the elderly Defender backed away and an angry, disgusted look fell over his face. He began to curse Joshua, and a withering barrage continued for some time. When it ended, the courtroom was hushed, and all eyes were on Joshua.

He leaned over to put some papers in a briefcase on the floor, and remarked, "Ah, just another day at 1201 Franklin Street."

It would be anything but.

All present were then called to rise as the Judge entered the courtroom and took his place on the elevated bench. Proceedings began with the non-Jury cases.

When my case was finally called, I stood before the bench wearing my Tallit. I felt a strong sense of peace.

With the Court Reporter transcribing, the Judge advised, "We are on the record in Cause No. 1670694 styled the State of Texas versus David Allen."

The Judge then called Dan forward—the Public Defender he'd first assigned, and who'd been so angry with me. He explained that as a formality, he needed to excuse Dan from the case.

I was then surprised as the Judge introduced a replacement—senior law partner, Brian Storts.

The day before the trial, Brian had happened into the courtroom. A long-time acquaintance of the Judge, he received an offer that most lawyers would have declined.

The Judge explained that there was a difficult "Pro-Se" trial the next day, and there would be no time to prepare, but would he be willing to help? Without hesitation, Brian said, "Yes sir, I'll do it."

The Judge then noted that Brian was not on the approved list of Public Defenders, and so would probably not be paid. Brian responded, "I said I'd do it. I'm in."

Brian's commitment would mean he'd have to rearrange a busy schedule of court appearances and appointments. Brian would keep his word, not for one day as everyone presumed, but for what would become two full days of trial. He was not paid.

As a baby, Brian took his first steps in a firehouse. His father and grandfather were firemen, as well as an uncle and numerous cousins. Brian grew up knowing that he too would be a fireman. But his father pushed him to pursue college and law school, and Brian obediently attended West Virginia Wesleyan and the Thurgood Marshall School of Law.

After settling in Houston and beginning a law practice, Brian's persistence showed up. At the age of 31, he completed the rigors of the Houston Fire Department Training Academy, and fulfilled his lifelong dream. Because his firefighting schedule is fixed, Brian can schedule court appearances and appointments as a law partner, around his "real" job.

Captain Storts is responsible for his own fire station, and routinely leads his men into fires and other emergencies. Remarkably, he is also married with 5 young children and is active in the men's ministry at Tallowood Baptist Church, where he and his family are members. Christian radio plays at his fire station, and it is not unusual to find Brian on his knees, praying with someone in the charred remains of a home or business.

Joshua's assistant would be Ms. [Stacey], the same attorney that had called my home on several occasions, trying to reach a settlement. Attractive and sharply dressed in a dark business suit, she would prosecute this case passionately. But, I sensed something troubled her deeply as she carried out her duty.

Stacey began by advising the Court that they had offered to me a "pre-trial diversion," asking only that I stay a certain distance away and "protest correctly."

The Judge responded, "I had mentioned previously that the State might be interested in offering a pretrial diversion—at which point I was soundly rebuked and rebuffed by Ms. [Kate]. I'm glad to see the State has modified its position on that." The Judge then asked if I were interested in such an offer.

He might as well have asked David if he wanted to compromise with Goliath. I had nothing but disgust for this giant that was accusing me, and I was here to watch it fall. How could I compromise with the very deceit that had taken my son Samuel 37 years earlier?

I again declined their offer and expressed the desire to proceed to trial.

Brian asked, "Would you like to talk to me first?"

I replied, "No, thank you."

Joshua, then introduced himself, and explained that he would be the lead Prosecutor.

He began by objecting to, "'Mr. Allen's people in the gallery who were wearing Pro-Life shirts, and to a certain woman holding a ceramic baby."

The Judge ruled that apparel was a first amendment right, but that the baby statue should be removed.

Mary put her baby on the floor just outside the courtroom doors, where it ended up being seen by people coming and going. When the Prosecutors saw this later, they demanded it be removed. A Bailiff was kind enough to keep it for Mary in an office.

Joshua then asked that I be required to wear my Tallit under my shirt. He explained that he was Jewish, and that he was offended I would wear a Tallit outside the synagogue.

While it may not have been in Joshua's tradition, there were no synagogues when the Torah was written. The Torah, in Numbers 15:38-39, directs the wearing of tassels representing the Word of God from the four corners of one's garments. For this purpose, the Tallit has tassels on the corners. Heeding the Torah, it was my practice to wear it whenever I felt led to do so.

Joshua argued further that it would play on the sympathy of the Jury.

The Judge then gave me opportunity to respond.

Horn of Samuel

I said, "Thank you, Your Honor. With all due regard for my Jewish colleague, I also claim Hebraic heritage. The Tallit represents a tabernacle covering of God's Word. It is directed in the Bible—in the Torah—that His people wear the Word of God, which is represented by the Tzit Tzit, [the tassels on the Tallit], from the four corners of their garments. I plead to the Court that I be allowed to be covered with what I believe to be the Word of God."

At this point, Joshua turned and glared at me, demanding, "You're not even Jewish! Are you?"

There was a tense silence as my emotions rose to meet his. Turning to face him squarely, I looked him in the eye, and spoke clearly and forcefully, "I am of the tribe of Judah—Grafted in!"

Biblically, those who have accepted Jesus Christ as Lord are "grafted into the vine." Jesus is the root of the vine, and from the tribe of "Judah." The word "Jew" is taken from "Judah." Being grafted into Him is the essence of the Christian faith, which makes one a child of the "King of the Jews" and therefore, Jewish.

The Judge then said, "And with that, Gentlemen, thank you. I will refrain from commenting on the Tallit. However, Mr. Allen, you are free to wear whatever religious garb you wish in this courtroom. Thank you both" And with that, He announced a recess.

CHAPTER 9
SECOND ATTEMPT TO TAKE MY JESUS

After reconvening, Dan, the public defender whose anger I had experienced at the Arraignment, came forward and asked to make a "Bystander Objection" to the Court's ruling on my Tallit. The Judge looked surprised, but allowed him to approach the bench.

Dan began, "I would imagine that you [Judge] were still in law school when the now District Attorney [Pat Lycos], then a district Judge, refused to allow someone who was not Jewish to wear a yarmulke [the skull cap or 'kippa'] during their testimony."

"This gentleman is not Jewish. He cannot prove that he is Jewish in any manner. And I consider it an anti-Semitic slur for him to wear [the Tallit]."

At this point the Judge confirmed with Dan that he too, was Jewish.

Dan continued, his face reddening with rising agitation, motioning with his arms and accusing me of wearing a "costume." He argued that dressing like a priest does not make someone a priest, and that such behavior should not be allowed in the Court.

Horn of Samuel

At this point, a Bailiff stepped up from behind, and tapped me on the shoulder, indicating that I should move over and make room for him. I moved over and he positioned himself between Dan and I.

Dan went on, closing finally with the emotional statement, "This is not a matter of free speech!"

I knew Dan was correct—this had nothing to do with free speech. It was an attempt to remove the protective covering of my heavenly Defender.

Dan's objections had re-opened the issue for Joshua, who continued, "This issue is likely to inflame some passions, and I think you're seeing that on display right now, Your Honor. And with all due respect, I would again renew our request. And if the request is denied, I'm going to object on the record, in order to sustain it for the record."

The Judge then cited the Cannons of the State's Commission on Judicial Conduct that would prohibit restraining someone from wearing religious garb. He also cited Constitutional freedoms of speech and religion.

In closing, the Judge added that he'd conferred with other sources to insure he was making the right decision, and said, "My ruling will stand."

"Thank you, gentlemen. If there is anything else you would like..."

~ 43 ~

Joshua stepped in again, "Your Honor, for purposes of getting this on the record. There is in the first row—again, respecting your ruling—I understand Your Honor's ruling with regard to the First Amendment."

"There is a gentleman in the first row in the middle. He looks about 19 or 20. He's wearing a T-shirt that says: "ABORTION, THE HIDDEN HOLOCAUST." He is obviously free to wear that shirt. I would simply ask that if he's going to sit in this courtroom during the trial and during [Jury selection], that he turn the T-shirt around."

The Judge replied, "I will not order that. I believe that it is his First Amendment right to wear that T-shirt irrespective of how it is viewed by others. I think that is his right, even in this place."

Joshua replied, "Just for the record, I'm going to object to the Court's ruling. My rationale is, that I believe it has the potential to—it's not probative of anything—and could inflame the Jury. So with all due respect to Your Honor's rulings, I want my objection on the record."

The Judge replied, "Your objection is so noted. Thank you, gentlemen."

The Judge then called a second recess.

The "Pro-Life" attendees would later share that each time the Judge ruled in my favor, Stacey would turn around to watch them, as if trying to catch someone in the act of cheering. As a group, they were praying intensely during this time, and containing their elation as each assault by the prosecution failed.

As I departed the courtroom for the recess, I happened upon the four-person prosecution team just outside the door. They were huddled like a football team planning a critical overtime play.

They looked surprised to see me, and all four straightened up and stared at me as I walked by. I smiled and said, "Hi, guys."

Meanwhile, two of the "Pro-Life" ladies were meeting Mr. [Jimmy], whom they would come to call "the Enforcer." Mary and Wendy were both passionate sidewalk counselors, committed to presenting pregnancy alternatives, and to sharing God's love, with people in tough situations. To me, they were both faithful angels of mercy, missing only wings.

While seated at different points in the gallery, both had noticed a stern looking gentleman among the observers. He stood out because he was very tall, and wore a stern, authoritative scowl under a smoothly shaved head.

Jimmy worked for the District Attorney's Office. He was assigned full time to assist the Prosecution.

When the recess began, he came to Mary, where she was seated, and directed her to leave the courtroom with him. Startled, she asked if he were an Officer of the Court, and he replied, "Yes."

Outside the courtroom, with her back against the wall, he leaned over and asked her to surrender the cross necklace she was wearing.

With palm extended, Jimmy said firmly, "The Prosecutor is a Christian, but she didn't think it appropriate to wear a cross in the courtroom. But after the Judge's rulings on religious garb, she needs one."

Mary said, "My answer is no."

Seeing Mary summoned from the courtroom, Wendy had followed them into the hallway, and was alarmed to see this man, well over 6 ft. tall, demanding something of Mary, who is 4 ft. 11 in.

Wendy approached and asked, "What's going on here?"

Jimmy then turned towards her, and demanded she give him one of the several cross necklaces she was wearing. She refused also, and they left.

Like all the prosecuting team, Jimmy was torn by this case. A retired police officer, He wore a red wristband and a lapel pin with two tiny feet, both "Pro-Life" symbols. He had 10 children, and like most fathers, was quick to share his wallet pictures. His family attended the vibrant Sagemont church on Houston's South side.

Jimmy later apologized to the ladies, and to Steven, explaining that he was used to going after "bad guys." He said he'd acted instinctively, just doing as he'd been told.

The next day, after I'd learned of the incident, it so happened that Jimmy, Mary, and I were crammed together in a crowded elevator. He was directly facing me and none of us could move. Staring up into his eyes, I said, "Now, you all have cleared up that little misunderstanding from yesterday, right?" He nodded, and smiled sheepishly.

Heaven's Trumpet Call of Liberty

Harris County Criminal Court Building
1201 Franklin Street, Houston, Texas

CHAPTER 10
THE PROSECUTION MOTIONS TO LIMIT THE DEFENSE

Returning from recess, the Judge explained that the prosecution had filed a three part "Motion in Limine" to block the Defense from broaching certain topics.

The first part requested the Jury not be told that the State had filed the motion. This was customary, and the Judge allowed it.

The second request was that the defense, "...not make mention of the legality or constitutionality of abortion itself...in addition to any discussion of...specific instances concerning abortion."

The Judge said, "That will be denied."

The third request was to block any reference to any witnesses' personal opinions or experiences with abortion, or reasons for opposing abortion. The Judge partially granted this, with the exception that such questions could be asked during Jury selection.

I asked if that would preclude me from sharing my own testimony, and he said, "Not at all." But, he went on to explain that the State would have the right to object, and that he would provide a ruling then.

At this point, Stacey rose from her chair and argued that the case involved criminal trespass, and not abortion. Concerning abortion, she said, "We believe that it is not appropriate or relevant to this case of a criminal trespass for the Jury to hear."

I responded, "Abortion is directly related to the circumstances of the case."

The Judge advised that he would rule on relevancy objections by the State when they were made.

Stacey continued, "Judge, for point of clarification, he's been told that he can discuss these personal issues without approaching you first. And the State just asks that before he gets into his personal experiences with abortion a number of years ago—that that is not relevant to whether he was on someone else's property."

"We're just asking that, before he gets into that with the Jury, that we approach the bench on that issue so you can make your decision then."

The Judge replied, "He has an absolute right to testify; and if he wants to do that, then I'm going to have to cause you to object—as opposed to stifling his speech before he engages in it."

Before recessing, the Judge outlined Brian's limited role in guiding a Pro-Se Defendant. However, in my faith, Brian was the "Armor Bearer" provided for this engagement by my heavenly Defender.

The Judge noted that he had known Brian for almost twenty years, and that he was a "top-notch" lawyer, who possessed the patience and demeanor to handle difficult cases like this. He also noted that Brian was familiar with the issues around this case, and that since Brian also serves as a city fire fighter, had dealt with this issue a great deal.

I acknowledged the limitations being placed on Brian, and said, "Brian will serve as my "Armor Bearer," And whatever happens, it is not his responsibility."

The Judge closed by saying, "This case will never make it to the appeals Court. Thank you everyone."

CHAPTER 11
JURY SELECTION

With the Jury selection process, or "Voir Dire," it is customary for the prosecution to go first, and Joshua's presentation was quite lengthy, carrying over into the lunch hour. There were twenty prospective jurors, and six would be chosen for this misdemeanor case.

Joshua was masterful in his presentation, and so thorough in presenting the prosecution's position and conditioning the Jury pool, that they were convinced I was a religious fanatic and ready to convict me without wasting any further time.

In answering his questions, they'd also expressed frustration with being there in the first place. And now it was past lunchtime and they were hungry.

As I stood to begin my remarks, I knew the Defense needed to be brief and light hearted.

After an introduction, I spoke of a Navy roommate that resented religious proselytizers that came to the door. He would tell them that he was a "Frisbee-tyrian," and believed souls were like Frisbees. When you died, your soul was thrown up on the roof to bleach in the sun. After it was completely white, you went to heaven.

They smiled and chuckled at my story, and it seemed to soften the extreme picture painted by the Prosecutor.

I then asked a few questions, but stayed away from anyone's position on abortion. I sensed that my heavenly Defender would assign whomever He pleased, with minimal assistance from me.

In closing, I expressed my appreciation for their service. I apologized that we could only accept six Jurors, and asked the rest not to be disappointed.

Days later, I received a handwritten note from one of the attorneys who'd come to observe the trial. He wrote that, while he didn't necessarily agree with all my views, he just wanted to say, "Well done."

I searched for his law firm on line, and found he had a blog. There, he'd criticized the prosecution for having requested a Jury, and said that when I concluded my remarks to the Jury pool, he wanted to applaud. This seemed to confirm that my heavenly "Defender" had been my help.

The Judge then recessed the Court for lunch.

The pro-life supporters and I enjoyed some spirited fellowship at a nearby sandwich shop, reveling that "David" was still standing. It seemed everyone was experiencing miracles, and had received some "lashes" for their faith. We sang songs and laughed, and all too soon it was time to return to the courtroom.

Both sides had been given a list of the potential Jurors, with their individual background information.

As Brian and I discussed the list, Joshua came over to speak with us. He offered his observations on about six of the individuals who had past infractions of the law.

As he spoke, it seemed to me those were probably the best kind of folks to have on one's Jury. When he finished, I said, "Those are just the ones we want."

Joshua looked shocked. Backing away and glaring at me again, he said firmly, "Mr. Allen... I am not your friend!" Then he turned and left.

Horn of Samuel

CHAPTER 12
THE PROSECUTION BEGINS

As the Court reconvened after lunch, I asked that my shofar be brought up, and the Judge directed security to do this. He then asked, "Why would they confiscate that?"

Joshua replied, "It's a weapon."

When Stacey attempted to elaborate, Joshua cut her off, and repeated, "It's a weapon."

My colleague had a better understanding than most. When the shofar blast is heard as God's judgment, it is a fearful thing. But for those who understand God's grace, it a joyous sound.

Stacey then said that the prosecution wished to invoke "The Rule" and would call all their witnesses into the Court for swearing in. I'd not given much thought to witnesses, and turned and asked the gallery, "Are you all willing to testify, Steven, Jonathan, Jordan, Mary, Wendy, Lloyd, Willie…?"

The Judge then explained that "The Rule" meant that witnesses are not allowed to remain in the Courtroom while the other witnesses testified, nor are they allowed to discuss testimony among themselves.

These friends were here to pray and stand with me during the trial. And I didn't want to be alone.

I said, "I have no witnesses, Your Honor."

Once the prosecution witnesses were assembled, the oath was administered.

There was then a long delay as the Prosecutors had some confusion over the large amount of documentation they'd assembled.

Finally, they were ready, and the Bailiff announced, "All rise for the Jury."

The Judge welcomed the Jury, and Stacey read the charges, "In the name and by the authority of the State of Texas, comes now the undersigned assistant district attorney of Harris County, Texas, on behalf of the State of Texas and presents in and to the County Criminal Court at Law No. 14 of Harris County, Texas, David Perry Allen, hereafter styled the Defendant, heretofore on or about March 18, 2010, did then and there unlawfully, intentionally, and knowingly enter and remain on the property of another—namely, [Lisbonne]—without the effective consent of [Lisbonne], after having received notice to depart and failed to do so, against the peace and dignity of the State."

Ms. [Lisbonne] was the security guard I'd passed on my way into the building. She worked for a private security firm and reported to Parenthood's Head of Security, Ms. [Larissa].

The Judge then advised the Jury of my 'Not Guilty' plea and advised them of the sequence of presentations to be made by the prosecution and the defense.

Stacey began with the prosecution's opening statement, asserting that I had crossed a line between my constitutional rights to free speech, and committed a criminal offense. She stressed, "It isn't more than a Class B Criminal Trespass. That's what it is. It's a Class B Criminal Trespass...This is the case."

She went over and over this same point, reiterating what Joshua had already stressed with the Jury pool.

Stacey went on to tell the Jury what they would be hearing and who would be testifying, and dramatically presented Parenthood's various accusations.

She closed by saying, "You're going to hear why they have security. You're going to hear why they were frightened. And at the end of the day, this doesn't come down to a referendum on what your beliefs are. At the end of the day, the State is going to have shown you the basic facts that Mr. Allen trespassed on a property that he wasn't supposed to be at. There is no more to the story. And we believe that you will come back with a verdict of 'Guilty.' Thank you."

There was actually quite a bit more to the story. The prosecution was doing all they could to prevent the jury from hearing it.

My opening statement was brief. I told the Jury, "You are really part of something a little bit bigger than a Class B Misdemeanor Trespass. There are some questions here of legitimacy, questions of qualification, and questions of ownership. And you will see the truth of whether or not a Class B Misdemeanor Trespass occurred. I'm confident that when you hear the whole story, you'll understand. I thank you for being here."

The Judge then advised the Jury that all the witnesses had been sworn in, and directed the prosecution to call their first witness.

Their first witness was the HPD Investigating Officer, [Kenneth], and after introductions, Stacey asked if he were the Officer that went to the scene on March 18th. He explained that the first thing he did was to call the Complainant, which in this case was the security guard. She had told him, "The Defendant came onto the property, pushed her out of the way, and went into the building and blew a ram's horn."

At this point, I felt the prosecution had failed in their commitment not to raise the allegation of assault. Now the Jury had heard it.

Fortunately, the ladies I'd spoken with just before entering the property, had been there that day. As part of the Houston Coalition for Life, they had an HPD "Liaison Officer" they coordinated "Pro-Life" activities with. They had told him days later, that there was no physical contact. Knowing these witnesses existed, the prosecution was blocked from pursuing Parenthood's false accusations beyond their statement at the Arraignment.

Continuing to answer Stacey's questions, Officer [Kenneth] confirmed that he had spoken to other witnesses, and then spoken to me by phone. He said he had recorded the conversation. This had been transferred to a CD and was entered as State's Exhibit 27.

The tape was played for the Jury, and they heard me answer his questions with an honest description of what had happened.

Stacey then said, "Pass the witness, Your Honor."

The Judge said, "Mr. Allen".

I said, "Your Honor, I have no questions. Thank you Mr. [Kenneth]."

The prosecution then called the construction superintendent who had called to me from inside the fence. Mr. [Ernest] introduced himself as the Superintendent and Project Manager for Meyerson Construction, responsible for overseeing the remodeling project.

Heaven's Trumpet Call of Liberty

    I found it curious that Ernest called it "Prevention Park" instead of "Planned Parenthood." The prosecution then presented Exhibits 1 through 16, and talked Ernest through a series of maps and photographs of the property.

    Responding to Stacey's questions, Ernest then described the events in relation to the Exhibits and his warning to me. He stated that I had responded to his warning by saying, "God bless you." After some further questions, Stacey asked Ernest to identify the man, and Ernest identified me by my Tallit.

    The prosecution then began to ask about safety on construction projects. At Brian's suggestion I objected and asked, "Is this relevant?" The Judge sustained the objection, and Stacey passed the witness.

    Exchanging greetings, I noted that Ernest and I were "construction brethren" and expressed the hope that one day we could build something together.

    Over repeated objections by the Prosecutor, I finally succeeded in learning that Myerson's contract was with "Prevention Park," and not "Planned Parenthood."

    I then noted from the photographs that the "No Trespassing" sign was a Home Depot-style sign, on a small wooden stake. I could not remember that little sign and I asked, "Do you have a clear recollection of when that sign was put up?"

    Ernest replied, "Yes. That sign was put up, I would say, after the fact."

I felt disappointed, and wondered, "Had the Prosecutors knowingly mislead the Jury with this exhibit?"

I asked Ernest if he'd ever identified himself as someone in authority, but he avoided the question. I pressed him, and he finally admitted that he had not.

After passing the witness, Stacey asked further questions about authority over the property and again passed the witness.

At Brian's suggestion, I asked Ernest if there was some confirmation of his authority over the property, such as a signed contract. He avoided my questions again, saying that upon signing the contract that gave his company authority. I asked again if the contract was available, and finally he said, "No sir. It's not available."

With that I said, "That's all I have. Thank you Mr. [Ernest]."

At this point, the Judge dismissed the Jury for a recess.

The Judge wanted to address the parties without the Jury, because the prosecution had been repeatedly trying to silence my Armor Bearer from stepping in to assist me.

The Prosecutors argued that since I had elected to appear Pro-Se, Brian should not be allowed to speak, unless I first asked him.

The Judge advised, "In an effort to ensure that Mr. Allen has his Sixth Amendment rights protected, I'm going to let Mr. [Brian] break in at any time…"

Stacey interrupted, "I just want to clarify for the record that I objected because it's my understanding that standby counsel is, indeed, standby counsel, and they are to be silent unless asked a specific question. And again, he waived his Sixth Amendment right to counsel and said he wanted to represent himself."

Brian responded, "There are times when Mr. Allen may speak quicker than I can give him guidance, or in the event that he is apart from me, and I may need to speak up. Apart from that, I'm trying to guide Mr. Allen to the best of my ability, as quietly as I can. But there certainly are instances where I would need to speak up."

The Judge ended the discussion by saying, "And I understand exactly what you're doing. I think you're doing a fine job, given the circumstances. Mr. Allen, I think you're doing a fine job. State, I think you're doing a fine job as well. But, the Court's concern is protection of the record. And, so, I'm going to ensure that there are no Sixth Amendment challenges that can be raised as a result of an inability of Mr. [Storts] to jump in whenever he feels it necessary to do so. So, with that, let's all just take a quick break and come on back and get started."

With that, we followed the Jury into a recess.

Horn of Samuel

A friend, Peggy, had called days earlier, and told me to gather and take five stones into the trial. She was referring to the five stones that the shepherd boy David, gathered from a stream as went to meet Goliath. I had gathered them and had them in my pants pocket.

Earlier, I had shown them to Brian, and at this point, he asked to have one. When I took one from my pocket and handed it to him, he held it as though it were of great value. When he asked to keep it, I felt honored to oblige.

CHAPTER 13
THE PURPLE SHIRT

After the Jury returned, the prosecution called Ms. [Lisbonne], the security guard. Under Stacey's questioning, she explained that she reported to Larissa [Parenthood's Head of Security]. Stacey had her step down from the witness stand and show the Jury from the photographs, where she was on March 18th.

Stacey then asked, "Will you identify him [the Defendant] by an article of clothing?"

Lisbonne motioned towards me and answered, "Yes. He's wearing a purple shirt with a scarf."

My shirt was light blue. I turned to Brian and whispered, "The color of the King!"

I was referring to the Biblical use of the color purple to indicate royalty. I had wanted to be covered by Jesus, the 'King of the Jews'. Brian nodded and smiled.

Stacey continued with her questioning, and asked about my entry into the property.

Lisbonne said, "He just brushed by me and kept walking into the building.

Stacey asked, "Brushed by you?"

Lisbonne answered, "Yeah."

Lisbonne went on to say that she followed procedures and returned to the security trailer to call Larissa.

When it was my turn to cross examine, I greeted Lisbonne and established that her supervisor was Ms. [Larissa], from Parenthood and then asked who her employer was.

Stacey interrupted and said, "Objection, relevance, Your Honor."

The Judge asked me, "What's the relevance, sir?"

I replied, "Authority."

The Judge responded, "Overruled."

[Lisbonne] then answered my questions and identified her employer as "Pentecost Investigation."

I asked if her security company was employed by the construction company or by "Parenthood," and she didn't know.

I closed by commending here devotion to duty, and added that she seemed like a very dedicated employee who had done everything correctly. I also stated that there were some people who believed the facility would actually become a "Birthing Center," and that I hoped she would come and share her zeal there.

Stacey then called Ms. [Larissa], and established for the record that she was Head of Security for "Parenthood."

She explained that her responsibility was to oversee the security guards and "monitor opposition activity."

Larissa advised that her office was currently at Parenthood's Fannin Street location, but that on March 18th, she was just leaving the new facility and had seen me arriving.

Stacey asked, "And can you point him out by an article of clothing?"

Larissa pointed to me and said, "He's in a lavender shirt, sitting at the desk [defense table]."

Again I turned to Brian and whispered, "The color of the King!" This was the second witness to see me covered by the King.

As the questioning continued, Larissa explained that when she got Lisbonne's call, she told her to call 911. Stacey's further questions allowed Larissa the opportunity to paint a dire picture of the threats and violence Parenthood had supposedly endured.

Stacey then used Larissa to introduce State's Exhibit 26. This was the YouTube video she'd e-mailed earlier to pressure me into a settlement deal. Larissa had taken it, and posted the video, showing me speaking and sounding the shofar.

Horn of Samuel

The Prosecution had set up a large screen TV for the Jury. The Judge stepped down and joined us to watch it. After some final questions, Stacey passed the witness.

I began with a greeting, and then confirmed that Larissa had filmed the video at the Fannin Street location. She stated, "It was taken at [Parenthood]'s current location."

I asked, "Current? Is it going away?"

She responded, "Yes."

Continuing to answer my questions, Larissa explained that the current headquarters at Fannin Street would close, and transfer with its clinic operations to the new facility. This would happen in the near future.

I then repeated the words the Jury had heard on the video. Freedom Lord to love. Freedom Lord to live. Freedom Lord to walk in the light of Your purpose."

Asking her if she agreed with my transcription, she replied, "Yes".

I went on to confirm that she'd filmed the video in February, a month before the trumpet call inside the new facility.

At this point Larissa tried to continue into other accusations and I objected, saying her comments were nonresponsive.

The Judge ruled, "Sustained".

I then thanked Larissa and said, "I want to thank you. You're a very special person; you just really are. And I thank you for being here."

Heaven's Trumpet Call of Liberty

The prosecution called its next witness, an electrician named Bryan. Joshua took over the questioning and had Bryan recount that he was working in a man lift, installing ceiling lights on the day in question. Bryan began by saying he'd seen a man with a horn or trumpet enter. He said it was the same man he'd seen on other occasions sounding the horn outside.

Bryan was overly eager, and got ahead of Joshua, adding, "...so like, we've been receiving threats."

Joshua advised, "Let's take this one step at a time. Okay? Alright, so the person you saw—do you see that person in the Courtroom today? Can you please point to him and identify him by an article of clothing?"

Bryan pointed at me and said, "Over there wearing a purple [shirt] with a white scarf on his neck."

I turned to my 'Armor Bearer' for the third time and we both smiled and whispered together, "the color of the King!"

Joshua continued, "Okay. Now, you mention you saw him carrying a horn. At that time did you know what it was?"

Bryan replied, "Not really, man. First of all I thought it was like a gun or something coming in."

Joshua began, "Okay. Let's talk about that. What made you..."

"Objection, Your Honor", I said, "I don't see what relevance this has to do with a Class B Misdemeanor Trespass."

The Judge asked Joshua, "How is this relevant?"

Joshua rambled at this point, "It's his state of mind, and it's inherently all about a trespass. He's on a construction site, where this witness will testify, and the Jury has heard evidence that there had been bomb threats. And it's a trespass…and it's a serious crime because of the danger that can be committed at a work site…"

The Judge interrupted, "I'll sustain the objection."

But at the end of his questioning Joshua asked again, "…And you didn't know what the horn was?"

Bryan replied, "No, sir."

Joshua continued, "You thought it could have been a gun."

"Objection, Your Honor." I said.

The Judge ruled, "Sustained."

Still Joshua continued, "You were scared."

Bryan answered, "Yes, sir, feared for my life."

Joshua: "Pass the witness, Your Honor."

I began by wishing Bryan a good afternoon, and confirmed that his testimony had begun with a statement that he'd seen a man enter carrying a "horn or a trumpet" and that it was the same man he'd seen sounding the trumpet outside the gate on other occasions. I was trying to make the point that he knew what I was carrying.

But Bryan would not cooperate, and despite the Judge repeatedly denying their objections, the prosecution kept interrupting my questions.

Frustrated, I closed by telling Bryan, "I thank you for doing your best and being here. Thank you."

At this point, the prosecution had three more witnesses poised to continue this line of evidence, and the Court swore them in and advised them of the limitation imposed by 'The Rule.'

The next witness was Mr. [Jeffrey] who explained that he was the electrical general foreman. He'd been working in an adjacent wall, and heard a trumpet. As Joshua continued, I repeatedly objected as to relevance and hearsay, with the Judge sustaining.

Without having seen the shofar being sounded, Jeffrey began saying, "I knew it was the guy because he stood out on the street and blew the horn. So we knew..."

"Objection" I said, "nonresponsive."

The Judge sustained the objection and Joshua passed the witness.

I greeted Jeffrey and asked if he'd heard the words spoken before and after the trumpet sounds. He said he could not make out the words from where he was. I thanked Jeffrey, and he was excused.

CHAPTER 14
THE VIDEO

It was late in the day when the prosecution announced that their final witness would be a "Protestor," who had taken a video of the incident. This was [the Lady] who'd pleaded with me not to enter the building, and warned I'd be arrested.

The prosecution had always known of this witness, but did not subpoena her until the end of the first day of the trial. It was this witness that had blocked them from pursuing Parenthood's allegations of assault.

My heavenly Defender had arranged for [the Lady] to be on that sidewalk, at that gate, on that day, at that moment. He was protecting me as I entered the very heart of Parenthood's new headquarters to announce Liberty.

He protected me while I briefly filled a dark place, designed for ending innocent lives, with the sound of heaven's Love.

For some reason, the prosecution had just decided to send Jimmy to her workplace with a subpoena. He'd taken the opportunity to show [the Lady] wallet pictures of his children. He'd also told her that the prosecution team was "Pro-Life," and deeply torn by this case. He offered to drive her downtown, but she elected to drive herself.

During private questioning by Jimmy, he told her that Parenthood was considering adding assault charges. She replied that this was not true, and to protect me, revealed that there was a video to prove it.

I'd been unaware that she'd used a camera to film me, from the time I entered Parenthood's gate, to the time I exited, including my passing by the security guard.

The video was on a laptop computer belonging to a friend of [the Lady]. Jimmy immediately called the friend, and informed her they were coming to her home to get the computer. The friend did not want them in her home, and chose instead to bring it downtown. Once in the prosecution's hands, the video file was transferred to a DVD, and brought up to the courtroom.

Because it was so late, the Judge suggested having [the Lady] appear the next day so that both sides would have time to review the video.

However, Stacey said that the witness had an appointment the next day, and asked to proceed with presenting the video to the Jury.

Horn of Samuel

The Judge advised, "Let's excuse the Jury and take a look at the video." Turning to the Jury, he said, "Ladies and gentlemen, if you will give us a few moments, we need to do some work outside of your presence."

The Bailiff announced, "All rise," and the Jury left the courtroom.

At this point, I felt badly that [the Lady], who'd pleaded with me not to enter the building, had now been subpoenaed from her work place to a criminal courtroom. And if I objected, she would be subjected to examination on the witness stand and forced to testify against me.

After conferring with my Armor Bearer, I told the Court there would be no objection to the video.

The Judge wanted to confirm this for the record, and he asked me again. I replied, "No, Your Honor, no objection."

Brian added, "Mr. Allen is definitive in his decision. We had a conversation confirming that. He is adamant that he has no objection."

I said to Stacey, "My concern is for [the Lady]. If you all don't need her on the stand..."

Stacey said, "That is our concern as well. She's the executive director of [Houston] Coalition for Life."

Joshua said, "Mr. Allen, here is the issue. Will you simply stipulate that we can enter this evidence without a sponsoring witness? Normally we would have to call the person who filmed the video to authenticate. If you are willing to agree that we don't need to call her that is called stipulation."

I replied, "I will stipulate."

After further discussion to insure I understood, the Judge asked, "So the State will offer the tape in front of the Jury, and the Defendant will not object. Is that my understanding?"

I confirmed, "Yes, Your Honor."

The prosecution then entered the video as Exhibit 28, and dropped their next-to-the-last witness as cumulative and unnecessary. They promised to play the video for the Jury and rest their case.

The Bailiff announced, "All rise for the Jury please," and the Jury entered and took their seats.

The Judge stepped down again, and we all watched the video on the large screen TV.

As the video played, it was clear that I'd walked through the gate and past the security guard with no physical contact, and on into the building.

Background noise from an adjacent rail yard interfered with the audio, but the ladies could be heard praying while I was inside the building. The interference then seemed to die down and I clearly heard the words, "...forgive us our trespass..." I smiled.

The film ended with me walking back out of the gate, waving good-bye to the ladies, and calling, "God bless you."

With that, Stacey announced, "The State of Texas rests".

Horn of Samuel

The Judge instructed the Jury not to do any internet research or talk with friends or family members about the case. All rose as the Jury exited, and the Judge directed a recess until 9:00 a.m. the next morning.

CHAPTER 15
AN EARLY MORNING WALK

Friday would begin with the Defense. Aside from a few notes and exhibits, I hadn't given much thought to how things might go. The Bible says not to worry about what you will say before your accusers in court, and that the words will be given to you.

"When they bring you before the synagogues and the rulers and the authorities, do not worry about how or what you are to speak in your defense, or what you are to say; for the Holy Spirit will teach you in that very hour what you ought to say. (Luke 12:11-12)"

Some were comparing this trial to "David and Goliath," which was fine with me. I knew my heavenly Defender was watching over me. It was an honor to face this giant, and I was looking forward to seeing it fall.

Arriving downtown early, and parking in a public garage, I donned the Tallit and set out with my shofar into the familiar grid of concrete valleys formed by the tall buildings of downtown Houston.

Horn of Samuel

Over the past 18 months, I'd been the coordinator for a group of two dozen shofar sounders. I'd seen the "sound of heaven" begin to flow in various settings. And, I'd grown to love this city as we were called to sound in and all around it.

I had come downtown frequently on my own as well, to sound the shofar and witness of God's love. Police, lawyers, businessmen, homeless, or students—it was always a joy to meet and share with those drawn to the "sound of heaven."

City Hall represented the heart of the city, and I knew it was beating with the precious "lifeblood" of the souls that traveled in and out every day on the "arteries" of its highways.

The shofar soundings had been concentrated around City Hall. There had been a nine shofar assembly around its reflecting pond for Rosh Hashanah [the Feast of Trumpets] the previous Fall.

The steady stream of "shofar miracles" I'd experienced would fill another book. I knew that Houston is special to God, and that it is destined for an outpouring of God's Spirit.

Recently, I'd also realized that this Goliath of deception and heartbreak would have to be brought down in the process of God's Spirit arriving. With an attitude of thankfulness for all my heavenly Defender had done so far, I found several locations to sound the shofar.

At 1000 Main Street, I discovered a marble monument. It formed an open window overlooking a reflecting pond. Deeply engraved in the stone above the window were the words, **"AS WE BUILD OUR CITY LET US THINK THAT WE ARE BUILDING FOREVER."**

I learned later that the identical words were engraved in the lobby of City Hall during its construction in the late 1930's. They come from an 1849 book entitled, 'Seven Lamps of Architecture'.

There, the author wrote, "Therefore, when we build, let us think that we build forever. Let it not be for present delight, nor present use alone; let it be such work as our descendants will thank us for, and let us think, as we lay stone on stone, that a time is to come when those stones will be held sacred because our hands have touched them, and that men will say as they look upon the labour and wrought substance of them, **"See! This our fathers did for us."**

While the words were being engraved into Houston's City Hall, a great holocaust was going on in Europe. Like the memorials of that holocaust, will Houston's surviving children one day gather at Parenthood's building, to grieve the loss of their brothers and sisters, and say, **"See! This our fathers did for us?"**

As these thoughts began to form, I committed the engraved words to memory. Surely they would help the Jury understand that the 'Giant' must fall.

As I sounded a series of shofar calls through the marble window, they echoed back reassuringly from the tall buildings that surround it.

Continuing north on Main Street, I came to an old hotel—the St. Germain. Its ground floor cafe and outdoor sidewalk tables were abandoned at this early hour.

I paused, sensing something familiar, and saw across the street a Gothic tower, the headquarters of JP Morgan Chase Bank. I'd sounded the corners of that building one evening about a year earlier. Now I recalled the applause and shouts of encouragement from the dinner patrons at these very tables, when they'd heard the "trumpet call."

Then I noticed something in the concrete planters on either side of the entrance; ornamental lion heads. My heart leaped—they represented my heavenly Defender—the "Lion of Judah."

I didn't understand then, but the marble window and these lion heads, would become significant later in the day. I sounded the shofar again and began walking toward the courthouse.

Arriving in high spirits, I was greeted with the embraces and prayers of a gathering of "Pro-Life" supporters and shofar brothers.

Heaven's Trumpet Call of Liberty

HOUSTON CHRONICLE

May 20, 2010
Planned Parenthood debuts new building

Its $26 million center in Houston is largest of its kind in U.S. --By CINDY GEORGE

Michael Paulsen, Houston Chronicle

The new center opened with a snip of the scissors by Mayor Annise Parker, flanked by Planned Parenthood officials Peter Durkin, third from left, Rita Lucido, second from right, and others.

"See! This our fathers did for us."

CHAPTER 16
THE DEFENSE BEGINS

The Court again had my shofar brought up from security, and I returned it to its place at the center of the defense table. The Jury had not yet entered, and Brian and I conferred. He'd had an idea.

Before the Jury was seated, I began, "Good morning, Your Honor. The Defense wishes to motion for an instructed verdict of "Not Guilty." The State has charged me with a specific allegation; that entry was made on this property without consent."

"The State has not proved that it was [Lisbonne's] property, as alleged in the Complaint; that [Lisbonne] was the owner of the property, as alleged; and that entry was made without the consent of the owner, whoever that is."

Brian added, "Specifically, Your Honor, the Complaint reads "...the property of another; namely [Lisbonne]. The State has wholly failed to establish that it is the property of [Lisbonne]."

The Judge asked Stacey, "Does the State have a response?"

Stacey argued, "Your Honor, in every criminal trespass case the State alleges, "The property of another." Possession is not ownership; possession is whoever has a greater right to possession of the property."

The Judge then asked, "Is this a publically or privately funded facility?"

Joshua answered, "Your Honor, I do not believe...well, I don't know the answer to that. You're asking a question with regards to the funding of "Planned Parenthood," the Houston Chapter. I don't know. But respectfully, Your Honor, I'm not really sure that whether it's a public place or private place matters much. This is a construction zone."

Joshua turned his attention to me, "He's an engineer. He brought that up himself in his own cross. He brought it up in his own cross that he is familiar with construction zones."

Joshua continued for some time, reviewing the list of accusations made the day before, but without addressing the Judge's question about funding.

He finished, "So whether it's public or private I don't think much matters. What's clear, Your Honor, is that he didn't have permission to go there; and certainly, it's enough evidence to survive a directed verdict and get it to a Jury."

With Brian's coaching, I said, "Your Honor, if I may?" Mr. [Ernest] did not have a contract. We have not seen it. We do not know who it was with. Further, the State alleges that the security was through a subcontractor. My understanding from [Ernest] is that he was not a subcontractor; and if I understand from [Larissa], she's the Director of Security, and that's who

[Lisbonne] reported to. So I'm confused, as I've been from the beginning, Your Honor..."

Stacey interrupted, "Judge, every day in this court we try people in criminal trespass cases. As a matter of fact, we had one yesterday. You took the plea on it. It was a construction site of a residential facility. I don't know who the owner is."

Brian stepped in, "Judge, we're on this case today."

The Judge, "One at a time."

Stacey continued, "This happens every day. This person went on the property. He was given notice by the construction person that he couldn't be there. Every single day the courts hear these matters. The person doesn't have to be the owner; it's anyone who has the authority, whether it's a security guard, or whether it's the property manager. It's not the owner that has to have the authority."

The Judge said, "The argument of ownership falls on its face with me. The issue, as I see it, is whether or not the facility is a publicly funded facility or a privately funded facility. If it's privately funded, then the issue of ownership falls on its face."

"If it's publicly funded, there are some other considerations that the Court has to take into account because the Defendant can bring up for the first time on appeal, a due process argument. And so to make sure that that's not an issue that has to be addressed later, let's resolve it now."

"I'll direct your attention to 209 S.W.3d., 296. Let me know how, and if at all, the Anthony v. State case plays into this decision; whether there is a curable due-process protection if it is a publically funded facility. I don't know but I do know that this issue can be brought up for the first time on appeal."

Joshua asked, "I'm sorry, 209 S.W.2d?"

The Judge, "S.W.3d.,296 Anthony v. State."

Joshua, "Is that the Opinion cite?"

The Judge, "I'll give you the key numbers: 110, 268, 92. If it flies—it may very well not. Let's litigate that issue at this point and key number 386, as well."

"We will readdress it at the time the Defense rests its case in chief, so you'll have some time to research."

Joshua, "I'm sorry; the name of the case was styled what?"

The Judge answered, "Anthony v. State."

The Judge then said, "We'll let the Defense go ahead and put on its case. If that case bears any relevance here, then I can readdress the issue at the conclusion of his case. If it does not, then we will have the evidence to put on and we can track forward with the charge to the Jury."

The Judge advised me, "I'm not denying your motion, sir; I'm withholding judgment at this time."

I replied, "Thank you, Your Honor."

The Judge responded, "Thank you, sir."

The Bailiff announced, "All rise," and the Jury entered.

The Judge stated, "The State having rested, Mr. Allen, would you call your first witness, please."

I replied, "Your Honor, the Defense would call myself."

The Judge asked, "Would you stand and raise your right hand to be sworn."

I raised my right hand and the Court Clerk administered the oath, "Do you solemnly swear that in the cause now on trial, you will tell the truth, the whole truth, and nothing but the truth, so help you God?"

I responded, "I do."

I began, "My name is David Allen. I'm going to present this morning, the reasons that the allegation of a Class B Misdemeanor Trespass in not supported. I will first of all commend the Prosecution..."

Joshua stopped me, "I'm going to object, Your Honor, to how he's going to present that this isn't a trespass. It's got to be relevant to the events of that day, so I'd ask Your Honor to direct him toward a narrative of what happened that day."

Brian said, "Judge, if we may respond. Mr. Allen has, in his mind, the formulation of his story. It is an expression of his state of mind at the moment [of the event]. I'm certain, after having talked with him, that his narrative will be related to the specific facts of the incident."

The Judge advised, "Please stick to the facts of the incident."

I continued, "The allegation is one of trespass. But there are instances where entry is made onto a property that would not be prosecuted as trespass. There are three that I want to discuss. I'll need some latitude to explain how the facts of this case relate to each of these three areas."

"First of all, legitimate purpose. If you have a property, and there is an emergency, and uniformed police or firemen or emergency medical technicians need to enter, they have every right to go in and do their job..."

Joshua interrupted, "Again, Your Honor, I'm going to..."

I tried to continue, "That's the first area..."

The Judge stopped me, "Hold it."

Joshua said, "Excuse me, Mr. Allen. Your Honor?"

The Judge responded, "Yes, sir?"

Joshua, "Again, I'm going to object."

The Judge said, "Sustained. [Mr. Allen] if you'll just tell us what happened that day. You can say all of this later in closing argument; but for right now, we need you to focus on what happened that day."

I said, "That day the Prosecution has done a wonderful job with videos and maps and charts and all their evidence. It was very well done. My commendation goes to these thorough and competent attorneys."

"In this case, what they have illustrated is that I walked onto a property, and sounded a shofar, and departed. And I have no other comment—[but] to confirm that, yes indeed, that was David Allen walking into that property and blowing the shofar."

Brian stood up, "I have latitude in the courtroom, but I ask permission nonetheless."

The Judge, "Yes."

Brian walked over and we spoke privately. He was concerned that my blunt admission might not be the best Defense strategy. As we finished, Brian returned to his seat, and I turned back to the Jury.

"That morning, I came with a legitimate purpose, and unique qualifications. For that particular moment. On that particular day. And that particular place."

"A place whose ownership has not yet been established. I firmly believe that that property is... "

I was going to acknowledge the Creator as the higher authority over the property, but Joshua interrupted, "Objection! Improper narrative and argument!"

The Judge, "Overruled."

I continued, "And that's what I'll present; evidence for each of those three areas:

- that there was a legitimate purpose to the entry of the property;

- that there was a unique qualification...that I'm blessed with; and
- that the owner [the Creator] of that property was not offended."

The Judge asked, "Do you have anything further, sir?"

"I have evidence to present on each of these three areas, and at some point, will need to go through this with the Jury. Is now the appropriate time?"

The Judge responded, "Yes, sir."

I faced the Jury and began, "In the presentation by the State, there was a YouTube video presented of me standing on the corner of Planned Parenthood and blowing the shofar. I have taken the liberty of transcribing the words in that video."

I was unfamiliar with the procedure for entering evidence. After reviewing my transcription, Joshua helped me label and enter "Defense Exhibit 1."

Then I recited the words from Larissa's video that I'd spoken a month before the "trespass":

"Freedom Lord, to live! Freedom Lord, to love! Freedom Lord, to walk in the light of Your purpose!"

"That's the message. It doesn't matter which side of the issue you're on. It's a message that everyone is entitled to hear."

"The purpose of my visits, as you'll see from subsequent illustrations, is simply to share this message, and to do it in love, and in a peaceful way."

"The purpose of the incident was legitimate. The purpose was just as legitimate as anyone else who would go in there to help."

"Before the shofar was sounded, there was a warning. And then the shofar was sounded. And after that, the message to the workmen was, 'Know that you are loved, and precious to the Creator'."

"And then you saw from the [Lady's] video, that I departed with a blessing."

"The purpose of entering that property was legitimate."

CHAPTER 17
QUALIFICATIONS AND OWNERSHIP

At this point I wanted to explain the qualifications I've been blessed with, to share the ultimate message of God's love.

I continued, "Now, Your Honor, I would ask for stickers [to label further exhibits]. I'm going to talk about unique qualifications."

I'd assembled 7 pages of pictures and newspaper clippings to illustrate my evangelism work, and to document some unique opportunities I'd had to proclaim the message of God's love, including:
- Leading a "March for Jesus" parade,
- A newspaper color photo showing where I'd raked the words, "JESUS LOVES YOU" in the autumn leaves covering a large hillside,
- A tent revival and my "You Are Loved" box truck,
- Baptizing "Joey" at Galveston after Hurricane Ike,
- Sounding with a group of shofar sounders, all wearing Tallits,
- A church flyer showing me leading praise and worship with my shofar and wearing a Tallit,

- A picture of my "You Are Loved" truck parked on a busy street corner, preparing for an upcoming tent meeting scheduled the following month.

I was unaware of the need to first share my exhibits with the prosecution, and Joshua corrected me. I handed him the pages to review.

Joshua said, "You're Honor, I'm going to object on relevancy grounds. May I approach?"

At this point, the Judge dismissed the Jury and we all approached the bench.

I began, "Your Honor, the District Attorney has gone to extraordinary length to request a Jury, and to present evidence; [28 Exhibits]. At this point it is essential to the Defense to have opportunity to explain the unique qualifications, the legitimate purpose, and the actual ownership of the property. I ask for your continued patience."

The Judge asked, "How does this information relate to the events of March the 18th?"

I responded, "It illustrates the character and the purpose of a message that's been consistent throughout my walk. It lends an understanding to the Jury, of the legitimate purpose and unique qualifications for me being there that day, at that moment."

Joshua countered that my package was not relevant to the events of March 18th, and after his further arguments, succeeded in reducing the 7 pages of "Defense

Exhibit 2", to the last two pages—the church flyer and the recent picture of the "You Are Loved" truck.

Still in conference with the Judge, we discussed my planned testimony about my participation in an abortion in 1973—and about my son Samuel. I explained that this would be important for the Jury to understand.

I said, "This horn is the sound of love—and it is the sound of my son Samuel. It is the call of love and victory that is the voice of my son. He's been given the voice that I took from him."

Joshua asserted that my faith and practices, and the fact that I'd been party to an abortion, were not relevant.

When he finished, the Judge asked "So your objection?"

Joshua replied, "Relevance."

The Judge ruled, "Sustained."

The Judge then explained to me, "You can always argue those things in your closing arguments, subject to the State's objections then. Let's keep things to March 18th, okay? These two pages will be admitted as Defense Exhibit 2."

At this point, Brian explained to the Court that another attorney [Mark] was researching Parenthood's tax returns with respect to the question of public funding. Joshua responded that the State would have a witness testify that, "There is no public funding at this time at all."

The Jury was summoned back to the courtroom, and the Judge directed, "Please proceed."

Brian said, "Your Honor, the Defense would ask that Exhibit 2 be entered into the record and that copies be provided to the Jury."

The two-page exhibit was entered, and copies distributed.

Addressing the Jury, I explained that on March 18th, I was acting as a minister. The two pages showed aspects of that ministry, one leading praise and worship with the shofar, and the other showing the "You Are Loved" truck parked on a busy street corner – proclaiming the familiar message like a billboard.

I explained that when my youngest son, Daniel, was 6 years old, he had the inspiration for the words, "YOU ARE LOVED." We'd put them it in big, bold letters on the sides of the box truck. I told them we'd then ministered all around Houston, and had used the tent for ministry after Hurricane Ike."

I added that, "While my education was in civil engineering, I am a minister. I go out in my faith. [The Bible], says to go and baptize. That's what I do. I go and baptize. And that's what I was doing on March 18th."

"As evidenced by Larissa's YouTube video, that was the message I delivered at Parenthood's new headquarters."

At this point I wanted to present the words I'd found that morning engraved in the marble window. This would explain that our city leaders should not allow Parenthood to build anything—much less their flagship headquarters and the largest abortion clinic in America—in our city. The Jury would understand we should not want our children to one day say, **"See! This our fathers did for us."** *This truth would surely touch their hearts.*

I began, "Finally, on the question of ownership. This morning I went for a walk in the city, and happened on a marble monument..."

Joshua interrupted, "Again, Your Honor, I'm going to object at this point in time, with reference to what he did this morning.

The Judge replied, "Sustained."

I tried again, "The question of ownership of the property..." but faltered, knowing the words would be objectionable. There was nothing left to do but pour out my heart.

I began again, "My Creator loves everybody equally; and it doesn't matter which side of this issue you are on—You Are Loved—and I'm here to testify because I've been touched by [abortion]. You'll hear about that later."

Horn of Samuel

"But God loves everybody. There's nobody that has any difference in standing before our Mighty Creator because of which side you happen to be on today. I know which side I was on [in the past] and I know which side I'm on now. And nobody calls me any names for where I once stood. I'm forgiven!"

"There are a lot of people in this courtroom, and on this [Jury], who have been touched by [abortion]—again, no judgments because judgment would start with myself. To be honest..."

That's as far as I got. Joshua said, "Your Honor, I'm going to object and ask that the Defendant and counsel focus his narrative on the date in question."

At this point I'd planned to enter as an exhibit, an e-mail blast I'd received, showing that many people understood on March 18th, that this facility would become a "Life Clinic," or Birthing Center to help women have and care for their babies.

An e-mail had gone out with the mistaken news that this had actually happened. I'd rejoiced when I received it. While it turned out to be wrong, this is what we were believing and hoping that day.

I began, "I would like to enter "Defense Exhibit 3," an unsolicited e-mail..."

Joshua asked, "Before you tell what it is, may I?"

I'd failed again to share my exhibit first with Joshua. I said, "I'm sorry," and handed him the e-mail.

After reviewing it, Joshua objected to the exhibit on the grounds of relevancy and hearsay, and the Judge sustained as to hearsay.

I continued without the exhibit, "On March 18th; understand what is being built at the scene of the alleged crime. My understanding, my faith, and my declarative statements were, "No!" This would be a "Birthing Center"—a place where young women could be helped with their babies, and people could come to help."

"Lisbonne and Larissa would be a part of it. It would be a Birthing Center where young women would come and find help raising their babies, or perhaps work with couples yearning to adopt. In any case, it would be a place for them to love their child."

"And that's just what this is going to be: A "Birthing Center!" And it's going to be a wonderful thing for Houston. There are people here [in the courtroom] who know what we've been declaring. And I 'm going to believe it today—what this facility is going to be."

"It hasn't opened yet. It's not anything yet. It's planned to be the largest facility of its kind—and Houston will be famous for it."

"But [my city] will be famous for having the largest Birthing Center—not the largest abortion clinic."

"So that's my faith. And on March 18th, that was declared [and in the days before and after that]. That's what I believed on that date."

Next I wanted to offer information from Parenthood's own web site, to demonstrate the intended purpose of the building, which included late term abortions.

This time I remembered to share it with Joshua, and with his help, labeled and submitted "Defense Exhibit 4." The Court distributed copies to the Jury.

I began, "Again, this building is not yet anything but a construction site on Highway 45 and Cullen. It is centered in four minority neighborhoods. This is what existed on March 18th."

"You may notice in the architect's rendering of the building, there is no wrought iron fence around it."

"If you look on the third floor—the third floor will have something called an "Ambulatory Surgical Center." And that's the heart of what this building is for. It will more than double the [current facility's] capacity, so whatever is being done there, can more than double."

"As the Prosecution pointed out, this trial is not about [abortion]. But that's [obviously] staring at us all here. He says this trial is about whether a Class B Misdemeanor Trespass occurred on March 18th, and this is the facility—this construction site."

I then asked for the State's Exhibits, and told the Jury that the "No Trespassing" sign the Prosecution said I'd ignored, had actually been put up after March 18th.

I said, "On that day it was nothing more than a construction site. [What it was] to be used for—its purpose—[was a matter of] opinion."

"My understanding was that it was going to be a Birthing Center—a place where young women would come for assistance. At that time it was not [an abortion] clinic."

"We still have not determined who owned it. If it's "Prevention Park" or if it's "Parenthood" or "Preventive Parenthood" or whatever."

"It has not been demonstrated that Mr. [Ernest] had any more authority than I did. There is no contract. We don't even know who the contract was with."

"The security guard—I'm not sure whether she works for Planned Parenthood, or the construction company, or for a security agency. I don't know. I'm confused."

I added that they should now understand what my hope and faith had been that day.

At this point my Armor Bearer wanted a private conference, and with his guidance, I reiterated to the Jury:

- That I'd seen no signs,
- The front gate was open, I did not sneak in,
- I did not know who Mr. [Ernest] was, and my reaction to his warning of arrest was, "Why are [you building this] in my city? I love this city.

Horn of Samuel

We're supposed to be building forever. Why are we building this?

The "You Are Loved" truck and tent being readied for a tent meeting on the corner of Beechnut and Eldridge in West Houston.

CHAPTER 19
THE TRUMPET SOUNDS IN THE COURT

I concluded, "What happened, happened at a particular hour on a particular day. The sound of God's love was brought down from heaven. I just wish I could blow the horn here for you."

"The purpose of blowing it that day was for a specific time that it needed to be done—done at that specific time."

"It was not a clinic. It was not anything but a construction site that day. Certainly, there is no justification for someone walking into any other type of facility and doing that. That would be a problem and I'm in one hundred percent agreement."

"I would note that, had I walked onto any other construction site in Houston, I might have been hollered at; but there's something more here. It's a matter of faith."

"It's a matter of faith because of the issue—because of the "tension" in our country. That "tension" has created something much bigger than any of us here. It's nationwide. It's everywhere."

"So, I had to be silenced. Something special had to be done for this Class B Misdemeanor Trespass."

"This charge has so many holes in it that whatever it was, it was not a Class B Misdemeanor Trespass." And I rested my case.

At that point, my Armor Bearer got up from the Defense table and walked over to join me in front of the Jury. He handed me an "arrow" I'd never thought to use, and returned to his chair.

I turned and said, "Your Honor, the Defense motions that the shofar be sounded. It's been alleged by the Prosecution that it is an alarming sound. But in fact, it is a wonderful sound. It is the sound of heaven's love. And I would ask to sound the shofar in the courtroom as it was sounded that day."

The Judge paused for a moment. I was actually surprised when he turned to Joshua and asked, "Well?"

Joshua also paused for a moment, and answered, "The Prosecution will agree...On the condition that Mr. Allen enter the shofar as "Defense Exhibit 5"."

I started to nod my head agreement, but Brian stood up and cut me off, "Your Honor! The Defendant is unaware that if he enters the shofar into evidence, it becomes the property of the Court."

He then paused, and added, "The Defense asks that a photograph of the shofar be substituted."

Joshua became adamant, and argued, "It's central to this case, Your Honor. I think the Jury needs to be able to touch and feel it. I have no objection...but only on the condition that it be entered it as "Defense Exhibit 5!""

Heaven's Trumpet Call of Liberty

The Judge pondered this for a moment, and ruled, "I'll allow a photograph to be substituted."

Walking slowly to the Defense table, where the shofar had rested for both days of the trial, I took a vial of anointing oil from my pocket. I poured some into the bell end and picked it up. As I rubbed the oil around the inside and outside of the shofar, I took a position under the Judge's right hand, facing the courtroom.

I didn't know it then, but there were intense prayers being offered by many in the gallery. Quincey was praying in Hebrew. Cindy was praying in tongues.

One man in the gallery was grimacing, his hands clamped over his ears, intent on not hearing the sound.

I spoke clearly into the tense atmosphere that filled the courtroom, making three announcements, pausing between each,

- **"This is the sound that was heard at Jericho, when God's people were being denied entry into what God had promised them!"**

- **"This is the sound that was heard with Gideon's small band, when a countless enemy was scattered before the army of God!"**

- **"And this is the sound that will be heard...with the coming of Messiah!"**

I then lifted the shofar to my lips, and gently sounded three broken blasts, that signified to me, the surrender of a broken heart to God.

Tau—Daaahhh ...Tau—Daaahhh ...Tau—Daaahhh

There was silence as I returned the shofar to its place on the Defense table.

I then continued, "There's a moment of silence after sounding the shofar, as each person deals with the sound in a special and unique way."

"But that sound is the sound of love. It is a wonderful Truth that we have—that we are each individually and completely loved—no matter what. No matter where we've been—we're completely loved."

"And this world, this nation, needs to hear that message. They need to know that message that no matter what, we are loved. No matter how things are economically, politically, morally...no matter what...we are loved."

At this point the Defense rested and a recess was called for lunch. We gathered at the sandwich shop and fellowshipped again in an atmosphere of pure joy. Returning to the courthouse, there was a sense of victory in the abandoned hallway of the court building, and we began singing boldly, "These Are the Days of Elijah", and "Sound the Trumpet in Zion" and other joyful songs of faith.

Then it was time for Joshua's cross examination.

CHAPTER 20
CROSS EXAMINATION

After the Jury had re-entered, the Judge explained, "We are back on record. It is the State's opportunity now, ladies and gentlemen, to cross-examine Mr. Allen. Mr. [Joshua], do you have any questions of this witness?

Joshua replied, "I do, Your Honor".

Beginning with some background questions, he then proceeded to my heritage.

Joshua asked, "You're not Jewish, are you, sir?

I responded, "Oh yes I am."

Joshua, "You're Jewish?"

I answered, "Absolutely."

Joshua, "And if you're Jewish, then, when is the shofar typically blown?"

I replied, "All the time. We get called all over the city to churches and events. And in our tradition, it's a joyful sound that people are discovering all over the world. People are picking up shofars and sounding them just because of the [wonderful] sound. It's a phenomenon that's truly out of this world."

Joshua said, "That's why you blew it outside the courthouse yesterday morning?"

I answered, "And all the other times I've blown it outside the courthouse, yes sir."

Joshua responded, "Back to yes and no, okay?"

He continued, "You've attended vigils at Planned Parenthood on Fannin before, haven't you? You're no stranger to the Planned Parenthood facility, are you sir?

I responded, "It's a new thing I've become involved in because of this new facility. That's what drew me. But I should have been there before."

Joshua asked if that were me in Larissa's YouTube video and I confirmed that it was.

Joshua, "Did you ever cross the line at the facility on Fannin?"

I answered, "I don't know what 'the line' is."

Joshua, "You never physically went inside that fence?"

I replied, "Correct".

Joshua then displayed "Defense Exhibit 3", the Parenthood web site information. He noted Parenthood's stated need for improved security. He asked, "You didn't have a right to go into that building that day did you, sir?"

I paused to consider his question.

Joshua interrupted my thoughts, "That's a yes or no."

I replied, "Yes and no."

Joshua, "Did you have a legal right to go into that building that day?"

Brian said, "Objection, Your Honor. No predicate has been laid to establish this witness is capable of a statement of what's legal and what's not."

The Judge ruled, "Invades the province of the Court and the Jury. Sustained."

Joshua, "Would you feel free to just walk up to any construction site and go on the property and blow the shofar?"

Brian: "Objection; calls for speculation."

Judge: "Sustained".

Joshua: "Are you aware of other hospitals in Harris County under construction?"

Brian: "Objection, relevancy."

Judge: "Sustained."

Joshua: "There was fencing around the facility, wasn't there?"

I replied: "Yes."

Joshua then related my walking around the fence, with my previous testimony of the Battle of Jericho, and asked, "In the Book of Joshua, didn't the troops encircle Jericho for six days without the shofar being blown?

I answered, "That's not quite correct."

Joshua retorted, "Okay then, please enlighten us. How many days was it?

I explained, "They marched six days, blowing the shofar. It was the seventh day that the shofars sounded and the people shouted."

Joshua stated, "But the shofar helped break down the walls of Jericho, didn't it?"

I replied, "In that case it was the physical walls, yes."

Joshua based his next question on the familiar children's song, 'JOSHUA FOUGHT THE BATTLE OF JERICHO'. He sang the part, *"And the walls came a-tumbl-ing down."* He asked, "That's what the song says?"

I replied, "That's what the Bible says."

Joshua accused, "You wanted those walls to come down, didn't you!"

I responded, "Oh, no. Not the physical walls. No sir. Those walls are going to be used for something [very good] shortly. We don't want to damage those walls, no sir." I was referring to the Birthing Center I believed this building would become.

Joshua, "You just don't want stuff to go on inside it?"

I answered, "I want lots of stuff to go on inside it, yes sir."

After some questions dealing with the warnings I'd received and my own reservations about entering the building that I'd shared in my testimony, Joshua got to the heart of what he had been repeating to the Jury since the Jury selection—that the case was only about whether there'd been a trespass.

Joshua, "Just to clarify, this case isn't about abortion, is it?"

I responded, "Objection, Your Honor. I think the District Attorney has asserted that it's not. I've not raised the issue."

"But if I'd gone onto any other construction site in the city, we wouldn't have all these District Attorneys observing from the gallery today."

In the gallery sat about a dozen attorneys from the District Attorney's Office, as well as other attorneys, there just to observe. My observation brought smiles and a ripple of laughter across the courtroom.

I continued, "But this is a unique experience, I think, a unique incident, with a unique issue behind it. But I've not raised that, and I don't intend to raise it. I told the Jury pool [during Jury selection] that it doesn't matter which side of the issue you're on. I didn't criticize anyone. I was expressing my praise that this facility is going to be a place of love and life and light."

Joshua said lightly, "I'd like to think the District Attorney observers are here because of my good humor."

He then became serious, "This case is about a criminal trespass, isn't it sir?"

I replied, "Class B Misdemeanor Trespass."

Joshua, "That's what it's about, right?"

I replied, "Yes."

Joshua, "That's the issue before the Jury, isn't it?"

I replied again, "Yes."

Joshua, "On the day in question, you went into that Planned Parenthood facility, didn't you?"

I said, "I don't know whose facility it was. Was it "Planned Parenthood Prevention" or "Prevention Planning." Was it a federation? We still don't know what it is. The evidence of whose it is…"

Joshua: "Objection."

Judge: "Sustained."

Joshua: "You went into a construction site, didn't you?"

I answered: "Yes, sir."

Joshua: "You didn't have permission to go there, did you?

I replied: "No specific direction to go, no."

Joshua: "I pass the witness."

At this point Brian wanted to conference. I appreciated his faithful support and told my heavenly Defender again, "Thank You for sending Brian."

CHAPTER 21
REDIRECT

After conferencing with Brian, it was my turn for "Redirect Examination." I stood before the Jury and began, "That day [March 18th] the construction project had gotten to the clean-up stage and begun demobilizing. They'd cleaned up around the fence, and from the Prosecutor's photographs, you can see there were no signs around that building."

"I understood from an e-mail…"

Joshua interrupted: "Objection."

Judge: "What's your objection?"

Joshua: "There was reference to a document not in evidence."

Judge: "Please don't refer to anything that's not in evidence."

I replied, "Thank you, Your Honor. My understanding on that day was that Parenthood was in deep trouble. That they had lost their funding and…"

Again Joshua interrupted, "Objection. That is, I believe, going to the substance of the documents not in evidence."

Brian, "That's a statement of his beliefs at that time."

Judge, "I'm going to overrule the objection. Go ahead, sir."

I continued, "We'd had a lot of people declaring that there's going to be life and birthing going on in that place. And in our faith system we declare things and believe them."

"Maybe they don't happen. I prayed for my mother to get better last year [from cancer] and it didn't happen. But we pray believing."

"So on that day, at that moment, I didn't know, and still don't know, who owns that property."

"When Mr. [Ernest] hollered at me, I didn't know who he was. And I replied to him, "God bless you" whoever you are. And I continued on around."

"And the ladies that were praying, that asked me not to go in—they weren't part of "Parenthood." They were a little reticent out of their love and concern for me perhaps. But they weren't in authority either."

"And, when Ms [Lisbonne] came out of a trailer. I believe she had a jacket on. I didn't see a T-shirt that said 'SECURITY'. And, I didn't see any signs."

"And that sign in the prosecution's photograph was put up later. I don't know why [they] put that into evidence—a sign that was put up after the fact."

"The only sign that was there was facing off to the side when I walked by it because the gates were open.

And the building doors were open. And there was no authority to tell me not to go. No ownership authority."

"I believed this facility was going to be something different. And it needed some love and it needed a certain sound in there. And I said, 'Okay, here I am, and here's this horn. And so the horn was sounded in there."

"I warned the men beforehand so they wouldn't be alarmed. I said, 'Gentlemen, I don't want to alarm you. I'm going to sound this horn.'"

"And they stopped what they were doing and stood there, and I sounded the horn gently, and I said, "Thank you, gentlemen. I know you're just here earning a living. Just know that God loves you. Each one of you is precious to your Father God.'"

"And then I left. And as you saw in [the Lady's] video, I waved good-bye and said, 'God bless you.'"

"Now, technically, I guess you can argue that's trespass, but under the circumstances of that day, at that moment, I don't think it was."

"The evidence that was entered, the YouTube video, showed my message, and that was the only message I ever shared there. Ms. [Larissa] has a lot more footage of me. And each time, I was telling her how much God loves her. I was telling her what a precious child she is. I just told her she was loved."

"And her video showed the message, 'Freedom to love! Freedom to live! Freedom to walk in the light of Love'. Now, I guess that's a pretty grievous thing to say in this day and age, but that's what I say. And people like to hear it. People come to hear it and a lot of people are encouraged."

"That was the message in February, and that was same message on March 18th."

"In closing, I'll just say that, on March 18th, there was nothing in my mind that told me I should not go through those open gates, and through those open doors, and into that building to sound the shofar."

"God bless you all and God bless this Court.

Judge: "Thank you, sir."

I took my seat with Brian at the Defense table and the Judge continued, "Call your next witness, sir."

I responded, "The Defense rests, Your Honor."

The Judge said, "Both sides rest and close?

Joshua replied, "Yes, Your Honor."

The Judge then excused the Jury and they left the courtroom. He then continued, "We're back on the record. I'll consider the motion of the Defendant while we've got the Jury out. I've presented both sides a copy of the Mistake-Of-Fact charge. What does the evidence show that [Lisbonne] said to…"

Stacey interrupted, "Judge, she testified that she went up to the Defendant and told him, 'Stop! You need to leave; you're trespassing on private property. You need to leave.' That was her testimony."

Stacey was mistaken. This had not been Ms. [Lisbonne]'s testimony, nor was it what happened. Ms. [Lisbonne] had said, "You get out of here you [expletives deleted]". And she was wearing a jacket over her T-shirt, as can be clearly seen in [the Lady]'s video, Prosecution Exhibit 28.

Brian said, "Judge, we'd ask to have that read back because I don't recall the testimony being the same."

The Judge replied, "I don't think Walter [the Court Reporter] can read back testimony written by another reporter. We don't have read-back capability right now."

"Our court reporter [Clarisia], for the record, had a family emergency and needed to leave. She does not have her computer notes here. Walter is a paper writer, like Phyllis. He could read from his notes physically, but he didn't take that portion of the testimony."

"The reason I was asking was so that I could fashion the Mistake-Of-Fact that I think has been established."

Joshua added, "The State has no problem with the Mistake-Of-Fact charge, Your Honor."

The Judge said, "In my language, [Lisbonne] had the authority to deny entrance into the facility. It raises an issue of fact as to whether or not "SECURITY" was exposed—the video will speak for itself and will show whether or not the T-shirt was exposed."

Horn of Samuel

"Another witness testified that it was by way of the T-shirt that this security person was identified, and so that's an issue the Jury will have to figure out; as to whether or not it was."

Brian said, "For clarification on the instruction, Your Honor, we would ask that that language be included—if she effectively articulated or expressed her thought to exclude him."

The Judge, "The way it's going to be written. 'Now, therefore, if you find and believe from the evidence beyond a reasonable doubt that the Defendant committed the acts as alleged in the information, and you further find, or have reasonable doubt thereof, that the Defendant, through mistake, formed a reasonable belief about a matter of fact, to wit: that [Lisbonne] did not have the authority to deny him entrance into the facility, which mistake and belief negated that kind of culpability required for the commission of the offense, you will acquit the Defendant of the offense charged in the information and say, by your verdict, 'Not Guilty'."

Joshua replied, "Your Honor, if I may. I'm not really sure that that's what he just testified to. I think that what he just testified to was that they had cleaned a construction site and therefore, he made entry and the gates were open. I don't think a Mistake-Of-Fact really had anything to do with [Lisbonne]. At least that was his testimony. I think his testimony was that he kind of thought, from what was going on at a construction site…"

Brian said, "If we can add, Judge..."

Stacey interrupted, "I was going to add to that. He also said he saw a man, but never knew what authority he had. He never said anything about the security guard."

Brian responded, "In addition to everything being cleaned up, which led to his belief, he articulated that [Lisbonne] had a jacket on and that he didn't know what her authority was, or who she was; that she came out of a trailer, and he didn't know."

Joshua had to respond, "I guess that it's really that he formed a reasonable belief about a matter of fact, to wit [Lisbonne] did not have authority to exclude him from the property; that [Ernest] was not associated with the construction site and..."

The Judge noted, "Well, [Lisbonne] is the only relevant player because hers is the name listed in the Complaint."

Stacey: "Well, Judge, in the Complaint that notice was given that he was told to leave by her."

The Judge then noted, "So [Ernest] doesn't really matter. It goes to [Lisbonne]?"

Brian: "We agree, Judge. If you wanted to add, that he believed on that day, at that time, that the property was open, consistent with the State's desires that we add that that absolutely has been a part of Mr. Allen's testimony of his Mistake-In-Fact."

The Judge, "I'm just trying to be as generous as I possibly can and I think I've done that with respect to this issue. I think, especially in a case where a person is representing himself, it is the Court's obligation to ensure that fundamental justice is done. I think that that's going to occur with this Mistake-Of-Fact charge. I don't want to go too far one way or the other. I think this is just right."

"With respect to the other issue that the Court raised, which was the issue of public versus private property, the Court has listened to both Mr. Allen and counsel, and the Sate, outside of the presence of the Jury—and off the record—to clarify what it is that the law says, and what it is that should be a determination in this case, where the State has cited a case, 135S, W.3d., 330."

"This is a case that deals with trespass on university grounds, and that if there's a clear statement that a person cannot enter into public property—public property can be trespassed upon."

"We don't reach that issue here because there's nothing to indicate that that Planned Parenthood facility is a public place in the sense that it is a place within a public/part-public domain. It's not that. It's a private facility. That's the Court's finding, based on the evidence that's in the record to date. I don't believe that the Defendant's due process rights were in any way infringed on, in that this is a private facility."

"I know that [Brian] produced some tax records that show—for purposes of the record, you can include those [Brian]—that Planned Parenthood is publicly funded, with the Court's understanding that these are donations from the public. And that while once the facility is up and running, there may be some Government funds that are also contributed; they are not necessarily what run this facility. They just assist in the conduct of whatever procedures take place in this place."

"So with that, we'll get the Mistake-Of-Fact charge typed up."

"Are there any other requests regarding the charge?

Brian added, "I've marked the 2008 tax return for "Planned Parenthood"."

The Judge asked, "Any other additional requests for the charge?"

Stacey advised, "No."

The Judge continued, "Anything else you want to put on the record or in the record before we put this charge together finally and bring the Jury back? Let's put all the case law in the record."

Stacey said, "Judge, the State is tendering to the Court <u>Spingola v. State</u>, 135S.W.3d., 330; <u>Griffin v. State</u>. It's a Texas—it's a record Opinion at Page 47; <u>Campbell v. State</u>, 626S.W.3d., 91; <u>Reed v. State</u>, 762S.W.2d., 640; and <u>Otwell v. State</u>, 850S.W.2d., 815."

The Judge asked, "How many minutes per side do you all feel you need to argue your respective cases?"

Joshua responded, "Ten."

Brian: "Mr. Allen has asserted the he would need about five or ten minutes."

The Judge, "I'll give you as much time as you need. If you say 'ten minutes', I'm going to keep you at ten."

Joshua, "That's fine."

The Judge, "Okay."

Joshua, "Ms. [Stacey] and I have spoken. Why don't we call it twelve minutes? I'm not saying anything about either side's ability to keep it to ten minutes. We'll work on that. Brevity is the soul of wit."

The Judge, "I'm inserting the Mistake-Of-Fact charge here and I'll work it in as I need in a logical way."

"So we've agreed fifteen minutes per side?"

Joshua, "Yes sir, that's correct, Judge."

Brian, "That's correct, Judge."

The Judge asked, "There are no objections to the charge as it stands?" Both sides affirmed this.

"Okay, let's bring in the Jury and we will argue the case. Both sides have rested and closed in front of the Jury. Walter [Court Reporter], you don't need to take the charge."

All rose while the Jury entered and was seated.

CHAPTER 22
FINAL ARGUMENTS

The Judge began, "Ladies and gentlemen, both sides having rested and closed, it is now the obligation of the Court to read to you the charge of the Court. This is the law that will govern your deliberations in this case."

"Once I finish reading the charge, the lawyers have requested, and I've granted, fifteen minutes per side for them to argue their respective cases. They may give you some of that time back but they have fifteen minutes, if they need to use it."

After the charge was read to the Jury, the judge continued, "The State of Texas gets to argue their case first. Once again ladies and gentlemen, closing argument is not evidence; it is merely a summation of what they believe the evidence has shown you. The State has the right to open but they may, however, waive that."

Stacey began, "Ladies and gentlemen, I told you yesterday, at the very beginning of this case, this was about a criminal trespass. You've heard a lot of information over the last day and a half, but at the end of the day, it's exactly what I told you it was—a criminal trespass."

"You're going to retire here in just a little while, back to the Jury room. You're going to elect a foreperson."

"This is the instrument that's going to guide you. What this is is the Jury charge. It's the law. This is the law. All of the elements that we talked about in "voir dire," [Jury selection] that we talked about in opening and that the Judge just read to you—this is the case."

"I took an oath to uphold the law and to seek justice. When you got in that Jury box, you raised a hand and you took an oath. And you told us in voir dire, that you were going to do the very same thing; that this wasn't about a personal issue; this wasn't about anything other than a criminal trespass; and you were going to follow the law."

"I want to talk to you a little bit about what the Judge read. This is something called Mistake-Of-Fact. Basically, what that means is that the Defendant wants you to believe that he was mistaken; that he didn't know if he was supposed to go in there that day."

"Now, come on. We know he told you he's a civil engineer. He told you he's been to over a hundred construction sites. He's told you he knows they're not open to the public. He told you that there are safety risks. He told you that he was driving up and knew he shouldn't go in."

"The standard for this is reasonable belief. You're going to read that in the law. That means, 'What would another person, an ordinary, prudent, in the same situation, think?' That would be any of those other protesters that were outside filming, and you heard what they thought. They said, 'Don't go in there.' Because they know and he knows."

"Ladies and gentlemen, make no mistake. This is not about anybody telling you that he is not entitled to his beliefs. I have personal beliefs that I have to follow the law, and so does Mr. Allen."

"Mr. Allen wants you to feel a bit of sympathy for him; and, you know, it's understandable if you do. But that doesn't make it okay for him to break the law. It's not about the issues that are surrounding the debate. The 'tension', as he calls it."

> *As with any protest against injustice, the authorities are forced by the tyranny imposing the injustice, to contain the "tension" it creates.*
>
> *"Tension" exists whenever tyranny's deception succeeds in passing unjust laws usurping the inalienable rights to life and liberty granted by God. Whenever tyranny gains power over a weaker group of people, it passes laws to condone its actions. It must then stifle the inevitable protests.*
>
> *The "tension" of abortion followed the U.S. Supreme Court's 1973, 'Roe v. Wade' ruling. It can only be relieved when the inalienable rights to life and liberty are restored to unborn children.*

It was not good for those protesting slavery when the U.S. Supreme Court enshrined it with its 'Dread v. Scott' ruling. It would take a bloody civil war to resolve the 'tension' of that tyranny.

It was not good those protesting Nazi atrocities and the laws they passed in the 1930's and 1940's. It would take a World War to end the "tension" of that tyranny.

It was not good for civil rights protesters in the 1960's. Segregation had been enforced by Court rulings, and District Attorneys and police were forced to prosecute those who opposed it. It was not until the abuses of that tyranny were exposed on national TV news that the "tension" was broken and those dehumanizing laws fell.

But after the "tension" of each tyranny was past, the "protestors" were esteemed. No one is arrested or prosecuted today for breaking those unjust laws—they fell long ago to the trumpet call of God's Liberty.

Stacey continued, "It's not about if Mr. Allen is a good, nice person. It's not about if he's sympathetic. It's not about where you fall on any of the issues that have been brought up in this case."

"It's about the law applied to all of us. The minute it doesn't, the minute it's okay for us, for the Jury to say, 'He seems like a nice guy—he only means love and good'—the minute we do that, we've all crossed that line with Mr. Allen."

"You need to think about the people that testified, the workers that were in that facility that day that heard that horn and how scared they were."

"Mr. Allen thinks he was just there for love, and maybe he was, but it's not okay to go onto someone's private property when they have told you not to, and it's not okay to go in and blow your shofar."

"You heard it; it's loud. If you don't know what that sound is and you heard about threats and you've been warned, and you're a 23 year old, up high on scaffolding doing your job, that's not fair."

"If you tell Mr. Allen, 'Well, you're a good guy, so we're going to let you walk away', then you've just joined him in crossing that line."

And the Prosecution finished.

The Judge said, "Mr. Allen, you have the privilege of arguing your case now. The time is 3:15."

I began, "Thank you, Your Honor."

Turning to the Jury, I began, "I've been advised to talk to the technical issues…"

At that point, I couldn't recall all of the technical issues. Brian had just briefed me on them, but I was tired and mentally overloaded.

I began, "The State…first of all, I appreciate these guys for putting up with people at their worst all day long in this courthouse. And every day they get beat up. So I appreciate the professionalism and enthusiasm of the

Prosecution and all these District Attorneys in the gallery. I appreciate your keeping our city safe."

"But in this case the burden of proof—which is the State's, I believe I heard—has not been met. There are all kinds of inconsistencies and problems. I guess I need to go through the technical part of this first."

"The pathway into the building was wide open. The signage was down. [The prosecution] tried to show a sign that was put up later. But, that was the condition that existed in the lunch hour on March 18th of 2010."

"There was a video that showed me walking into the building and not remaining, but walking back out again. And [Lindsey]'s assertion that authority was clear from a T-shirt. If you have a moment, go back and look at that video. There was no T-shirt with 'SECURITY' on it."

"You have that evidence. [The Prosecution] ran out and got that at the last minute by subpoena—so this must important. No uniform. There was never anyone that said, 'I am in charge of this property, and you are not to be here.'"

I'd tried to relay everything Brian had just coached me on, but I knew it was not going well. I prayed, "Take it Lord."

Continuing, I said, "Okay, now, that said, let's look at the legitimacy of why I entered and sounded the horn. What was the legitimate purpose?"

"It was a message, that, oh so badly needed to be heard. It was a message of love."

"And I was uniquely qualified to deliver that message. Several years ago, I cashed out a retirement account and bought a truck and a tent. And we've been using it to minister this message. We also used it for ministering to hurting people after Hurricane Ike. We worked in Galveston, baptizing there."

"The message on the side of the truck is, "YOU ARE LOVED." And so, with that experience, I was uniquely qualified to go in and minister in a place that sorely needs ministering."

I continued, "And now to the question of ownership. [The Prosecution] has not shown us yet who owns that property. There was a contract that Mr. [Ernest] mentioned. We still don't have that contract. We still don't know who the owner is. We generally know [Parenthood] as an 'ethereal' entity—it's actually a federation, and comes under a worldwide federation. It's a very unusual situation."

"Back to the 'tension.' There is a 'tension' in this courtroom. It is the same 'tension' we see whenever the inalienable rights granted by our Creator, are violated. We are created with, and given by Him, the rights to life and liberty and the pursuit of happiness."

"Slavery is a gross example. According to court rulings and laws, it was enshrined in this nation. Until the 'tension' became so great that someone said, 'This isn't right.' And I don't know anyone today that says we need to go back and reinstitute those laws."

"After that, something else took over—it was called discrimination. It too was codified into law and court rulings, and this same group of people continued to be treated differently and suppressed in their rights to life, liberty and happiness. And there were laws and attorneys that told us it was okay."

"We have 'tension' whenever we ignore what the Creator says, and take away the rights of a group of people, and say they are less. Then, you are going to have 'tension.' You can look at the death camps in Nazi Germany—whatever example you want to look at."

"When one group is subjected, and told, 'You don't have certain rights because we're bigger and stronger than you, there is 'tension.' And this is the 'tension' here today."

"Again, I'm not condemning one side or the other. Both sides are guilty of violence and extreme statements—and that's not the issue here."

"But with the civil rights example, it got to such a point of 'tension' that people right here in this city, some young men and women said, 'This isn't right!' And, 'We're going to go ahead and sit at this lunch counter.'"

"And that happened right here in Houston, Texas. And they were arrested and fingerprinted and photographed and booked and processed. And the Prosecutors did their job and prosecuted them."

"But it couldn't last, once people saw it and understood."

"I don't know of anyone today that says we need to have those [segregation laws] in place again. We've come a long way, but we've got a ways to go because we're human."

"And so there is 'tension' is here today. I didn't put it there. It's not my fault. The crime here is not a 45 second trespass. The crime here is that the message of this horn was sounded. That's the real crime."

"And that's why they need you to find me guilty of 'trespass.' But again, this sound needs to be heard. All these people who came to watch, they know. I didn't invite them. They came because this issue is important to them."

"I'm so happy that the sound is here—that I can share the good news of the Freedom I have been given, and to share my faith. I have a new way of putting it out there, and it is a joyful thing. You just don't know how joyful it is."

"Now, finally, I just want to thank the city of Houston. This is a wonderful city. This is a special city. I've lived here for almost ten years now. I'm not going anywhere because every tribe and tongue is represented here."

"I love this city. I want to share some words I found this morning, that are engraved in this city:

AS WE BUILD OUR CITY LET US THINK THAT WE ARE BUILDING FOREVER

"So I'm here to help build this city. And I've been doing my job and paying my taxes. I'm not the one who has trespassed here. Someone else is trespassing—doing something that does not benefit the city of Houston."

And now I wanted to share the real qualification that I had to sound heaven's love in the lobby of the largest abortion clinic in the Western hemisphere. The Prosecution had blocked the testimony about my son Samuel, since before the trial began, but now it was time. I would begin by telling them about a memorial where people who have experienced abortion can have a dedication performed for their lost children.

"There is a memorial in Chattanooga, Tennessee. I'm going to put my..."

Joshua interrupted for the final time, "At this point, I'm going to object as improper argument."

The Judge said, "Overruled."

So here was my opportunity. The way ahead was clear. The Prosecutors could not stop me from sharing my son Samuel with the Jury. And my taking away Samuel's God-given right to life in 1973. And God's forgiveness in 1992, that allowed me the honor of being on the front lines of the battle.

And then I lost it. With the objections silenced, and the way ahead clear, my mind went blank. My only thought was that it was time to rest the case.

I said, "That's all. We're not going to solve this issue today. There's enough wrong with this case that I believe you are going to throw it out. You're going to be under a lot of pressure to find me guilty. But I believe there's going to be a 'Not Guilty' verdict, and I want to thank you in advance."

"And if that's not your verdict, that's okay too, because the guys at the lunch counter—they didn't always win—so that's okay. It's up to you, and you have my endorsement whichever way you find."

"But a 'Not Guilty' verdict today will say something very loudly—it will get out, and people are going to hear it."

"If we have a 'Guilty' verdict, the Deceit that's behind this 'tension,' that forces Prosecutors to do this—it's going to say, 'We got him!'"

Horn of Samuel

"It's not [Joshua or Stacey]—there's something bigger here than a Class B Misdemeanor Trespass. So a 'Guilty' verdict will tell the world that this Deceit still has control."

"But our right to protest—it was a hard won right. A lot of people served a lot of time in jail to win the right to stand out on the sidewalk and say, 'No'."

"And, now to close. A 'Not Guilty' verdict, I believe says—and you can say it based on technicalities—or you can say it politically—or however it gets said—'We are not afraid. We are not going to compromise. We are not going to sign any kind of deal. We're going to go out and take our lumps until the world sees the Light and the Truth."

"So I just thank everyone here for being a part of this day. And I rest my case. Thank you."

The Judge said, "Thank you, Mr. Allen. Mr. [Joshua]?"

Joshua began, "I want to go through three things with you. What did you hear? Why are you here? And, where do you go from here?"

"What did you hear? You heard a case. Ms. [Stacey] and I put out everything. You told me in voir dire you expect there to be a thorough investigation by the police and the kind of evidence you'd want to hear in a criminal trespass case. That's what you told me."

"You told me you would want to hear from witnesses. You got it."

"You would want to hear an audio statement from the Defendant. You got it."

"Even better, if the statement came with a confession. You got it."

"Video would be good. You got it."

"He confessed! He confessed! He even told you on the stand this is not about abortion. This is about criminal trespass. That is what this is about."

"You told me in voir dire you recognized the distinction—that there's no distinction between someone's private home where there's a trespass, or if it's a corporation. You told me it didn't matter. You told me you understood that trespassing will create 'tension.' People will get upset."

"I gave you a scenario in voir dire. The scenario was that someone really felt in their heart of hearts that this is the most important issue facing our society and our country and said, 'please listen to me', and you said all that didn't matter."

"Even if it involves unborn children, you said it didn't matter. Everything you expected us to bring was brought to you."

"So why are you here? You're here because the Constitution of the United States gives Mr. Allen the right to a Jury. It gives him the right to a trial. He wanted his trial."

Horn of Samuel

"Now look, Mr. Allen seems like a very nice guy. And in some strange way now, our paths have intersected here. He came to Houston ten years ago and I came to Houston 10 years ago. We both came here planning on staying. We both love the city, both love the community."

"He came here, these last two days, because, make no mistake, something very special happened to Mr. Allen some years ago. He had a religious awakening. God bless him for it. I am glad that he has found meaning in his life. Not everyone has."

"Good for him. I'm happy for him. So is Ms. [Stacey]. So is the State of Texas. So is the District Attorney's Office."

"It doesn't matter."

"But the reason he wanted his trial—Mr. Allen is not crazy. He's smart. He's an educated engineer, who is a professional protester."

"He knew the rules of engagement. He circled that facility. He was waiting to go in. He knew what he was doing. He knew what he was doing! Even on the way over, he said to himself, 'No, No, No.' He knew it was wrong."

At this point Joshua had become visibly angry. No Class B Misdemeanor Trespass in the history of Houston had ever drawn this much passion. And his attack had now grown personal. And was about to get much more personal.

Joshua continued, "He knew he was going to cross that line and he was circling because he was looking for his opportunity to bring those walls 'a-tum-bl-ing down'."

"With all due respect for Mr. Allen, and this part is hard for me folks—in case you couldn't tell. In order to spread his message, he adopted some of the most important and precious elements of the Jewish faith."

"On Rosh Hashanah, it is the Cantor's job to blow the shofar. Only the Cantor!

Joshua was wrong. The Cantor leads the congregation in prayer along with the rabbi. The Cantor is a key position because of the important role music plays in Jewish worship. Professional Cantors are accomplished in musical arts and have attended Cantorial School and been ordained.

But it is the Ba'al Tekia, or 'Master of the Blast', an appointed expert, who blows the shofar. The position and duties are separate from the Cantor. While it is not unheard of for a Cantor to sound the shofar, Joshua was wrong in saying, "only the Cantor" sounds the shofar.

Joshua continued, "As a little kid in Hebrew school, we couldn't wait till Rosh Hashanah because we actually got to see the shofar blown. It is so special that it is only sounded once a year."

Horn of Samuel

The shofar appears throughout the Bible, in calling assemblies, in announcements, in warnings, in warfare, for coronations, praise, and many other purposes. While Rosh Hashanah or 'Day of the Trumpet' is certainly central, Joshua was wrong in saying its sounding, "comes only once a year."

Joshua continued, "I think he blows it everywhere. Everywhere! Why?"

"Because this is calling attention to himself, okay? This is his stage. You are his audience."

"He has his views on reproductive rights. I don't care what they are. Ms. [Stacey] doesn't care what they are. The District Attorney's Office doesn't care what they are, okay?"

"I told you in voir dire—I don't care what they are! Everyone has an opinion, okay? It is the proverbial third rail of electoral politics and cocktail conversation everywhere, okay?"

"You don't go there, because everyone has an opinion; it doesn't matter! And you all told me in voir dire; that it didn't matter. A trespass is a trespass."

"Where do you go from here? Where you go from here is back in the Jury room and look at the charge. The law is straightforward. Everything we told you in voir dire, you said you understood."

"Ms. [Lisbonne] had a greater right to possession at that property. She's a security guard. We've got the video of him standing by the security guard gate; he'd been told, 'Don't go in there'."

"He went in anyway. She said something to him that he chose to ignore. He went into an active construction site, and as a professional engineer, he knew better."

"Where you're going now is the Jury room. You have the charge. Read through it, okay? It's important to the State of Texas."

"But just consider this as you go back in there folks. You all told me you don't get a free pass based upon your beliefs. I ask you to remember that because it's what a 'Not Guilty' message is going to give him."

"And he entered this as a Defense Exhibit—it's from Planned Parenthood's web site. It talks about reproductive rights. It talks about other things, too— human papillomavirus, pap smears, HIV. [Abortion] is only a small part of what they do there."

Joshua was finishing by speaking out in support of the very issue he'd blocked the Defense from discussing. And he was presenting the same deceptive arguments used by the abortion industry. With no opportunity for the Defense to counter, the "Giant's" deceit was entered into the record.

Joshua continued, "If you give him a "Not Guilty." you know where he's going after this? He's going right back there. He's going to blow that shofar again."

"He's going to go there on Monday, and he's going to go there on Tuesday, and Wednesday, and Thursday, and Friday. And people are going to follow him because he got a free pass today."

Joshua was correct this time. I would continue going there and blowing the shofar. And many people would be encouraged. And their numbers would grow. And the message would continue to reverberate through the very "Giant" of the abortion industry.

"Freedom to love! Freedom to live! Freedom to walk in the light of our Creator's love!" And the walls of deception that Parenthood has built around our nation and around the world, will indeed come"a-tum-bl-ing down."

No objections. Go Joshua, Go! Your namesake, the Biblical Joshua, also directed the shofar be blown that brought down the walls of Jericho. And God's people entered into the land that God had promised them. Say it louder, Joshua!

The story of Jericho's walls is told in the book of "Joshua." And the modern day walls are indeed coming down—and all of those who, like me, who have worn the chains of guilt for violating the God-given rights of our children, will be set free. Free to experience and share our grief. Free to take our places on the battle front. The darkness is fleeing. It cannot stand against the Light of heaven.

At this point, Joshua was rambling, "It's a hard case. On the law it's easy. In terms of these other attendant issues, it's harder; I'll admit. It's harder."

"He's a nice guy. But there's a bigger issue here. It's not whether he's a nice guy or not. It's upholding the law and the private property rights that also exist in the Constitution of the United States alongside the right of freedom of expression and freedom of speech and the right to lawful assembly."

"Mr. Allen, in his closing, talked about the lunch counter sit-ins here in Houston. I will leave it to the judgment of history as to whether the fight over Reproductive Rights rises to the level of importance that the civil rights movement did in the 1960's."

"But just remember this; Dr. King's 'Letter from Birmingham' was written from the Birmingham jail."

My jaw dropped. Incredulously, I turned to my Armor Bearer and whispered, "Did he just say that Martin Luther King should have been in jail?"

Horn of Samuel

Brian looked as shocked as I felt. He nodded slowly saying, "I think so."

In this context, it must be mentioned that at one time in America, the Judge's ancestors had been slaves, owned and treated like animals. And this was done under the protections of American law and Supreme Court rulings. And only a generation ago, the Judge's family had known the oppressive heartbreak of their children being told they could not go to the same amusement parks as other children, because they were considered "less" human.

Joshua had essentially said that Dr. King, a shining ray of God's Love in the dark struggle of segregation, who had sounded a mighty trumpet call with his famous "Letter from Birmingham Jail," was "rightfully" in jail because of his resistance to those unjust laws—this hero who had led peaceful demonstrations that brought down the walls of segregation, and ended the physical and spiritual abuses of generations of men, women and children.

Wrong again Mr. Prosecutor. Those laws were unjust, and they fell long ago to the 'trumpet call' of Liberty. And this same trumpet call is sounding now against what you just called, "Reproductive Rights." This deceptive term is used by Parenthood to justify denying God's inalienable "Right to Life" *to unborn innocents who have no voice, no due process, and no appeal.*

Joshua continued, "Rightly or wrongly, whether he realized it or not, Mr. Allen chose to engage in civil disobedience; and when you do that, you understand the risks involved. He made a choice. The choice he made was to call attention to himself. His cause was to break the law."

The Judge said, "You have two minutes."

Joshua: "Thank you, Your Honor. So what I'm asking you today is to take all the time you need. When you do, I'm confident you're going to return a verdict of 'Guilty'."

"And I want to thank you all for your time and attention that you have spent over the last two days on this unique, special, and important case, and dealing with the right of a private property owner to protect their property. Thank you all."

The Judge said, "Thank you Mr. [Joshua]. Ladies and gentlemen, please retire to the Jury room until you have reached a unanimous verdict."

With that, we rose and the Jury retired.

CHAPTER 23
THE VERDICT

While the Jury met to reach their verdict, I sat in the gallery and fellowshipped with the "Pro-Life" and shofar brethren. There was an atmosphere of victory and celebration. David had faced the "Giant," and now it was time to watch the giant fall!

It was now clear to me why this trial could not be delayed. In several hours, Parenthood would begin a gala dinner celebration, with its leading supporters in tuxedos and formal gowns. They would toast not only their soon-to-open abortion mega-clinic, but also their 75th anniversary.

The event would be held less than 2 blocks from the courthouse, at the old Corinthian Hotel on Fannin Street. Nearby, hundreds of "Pro-Life" supporters were gathering to march to the Corinthian and proclaim, "Liberty!"

Parenthood would be celebrating 75 years of oppressive deception, and its largest abortion clinic ever, in the heart of my city. They would ignore the suffering of millions of women and men, hurting physically and emotionally.

Heaven's Trumpet Call of Liberty

And I would have the high honor of being there to sound the trumpet call, announcing that the giant had fallen.

It was only a brief time before we were summoned to return to our seats.

The Judge advised, "We have a verdict, ladies and gentlemen. I would caution you first, that whatever your feelings with respect to the verdict, not to engage in any emotional outbursts. However, while I would not be happy about that, I will not hold you in contempt. Let's bring in the Jury."

All rose while the Jury was seated, and an envelope was relayed to the Judge for his review, and then back to the Jury Foreman.

The Judge then said, "Madam Foreman and Mr. Allen, would you stand, please."

"Will you read the verdict to the Defendant please, ma'am?"

Madam Foreman said, "We, the Jury, find the Defendant...'Guilty'."

At the word 'Guilty', I felt my breath taken away. But instantly, I knew what to do. Turning to my Armor Bearer, I whispered, "Praise God!"

The Judge then polled the Jury to confirm a unanimous decision, and advised, "Thank you, ladies and gentlemen. Your participation is concluded. As I stated before, punishment will be decided by the Court. Thank you very much for your Jury service."

"We will address punishment as soon as we get back from talking with the Jury." At that point the Judge, Joshua, Stacey and Brian left the courtroom to debrief with the Jury.

Upon their return, we all approached the bench.

The Judge began, "Let's go on the record. The Jury, having found you 'Guilty' sir, do you have anything further to say on the issue of punishment?"

I answered, "No, Your Honor."

The Judge asked, "Does the State have anything further to say?"

Joshua replied, "No, Your Honor."

The Judge said, "There being nothing further to say, it is the order of this Court then sir, that you serve 30 days in the Harris County Jail."

"That will be probated for a period of six months. I have to assess some jail time in order to probate the sentence, and that will be six months probation."

The Judge was essentially saying that there would be no jail time. It was changed to probation.

The Judge continued, "There will be no fine, no court costs, no supervisory fees at all. There will be no community service, no drug or alcohol evaluation, no travel restrictions. You will have to get an Offenders ID badge."

The Judge continued, "I will be your probation officer, sir, so you won't have to go to the probation department. You just come to the Court, to me, and we'll talk every now and again."

I asked Brian if it were unusual for a Judge to assign himself as a probation officer. He smiled and said, "It's unprecedented." When I asked the Clerk when my first probation meeting would be. She laughed, waved her hand, and said, "You don't get it, do you?"

The Judge continued, "The one condition is that you remain 15 feet from the entrance of any "Planned Parenthood" facility."

"With respect to your right to sound the shofar, you may do that. With respect to your ability to pray, quietly or loudly, I say, 'Pray On!'"

HARRIS COUNTY, TEXAS	
OFFENDER IDENTIFICATION CARD	
ALLEN,	DAVID
SPN: 02486777	
DOB: 00/00/54	
Probation Term:	
04/30/10 to	10/29/10
Court: 014 County Criminal Court	
Offense: CRIMINAL TRESPASS	
Cause: 1670694	

CHAPTER 24
THE LION OF JUDAH

In the early evening hour, we prayed outside the court building, solaced in our spirits that a faithful witness had been made by all. But there was a deep ache. Our joyful expectations of seeing the "Giant" fall had been crushed.

We discussed whether we should join the "Pro-Life" march to the Corinthian. Having anticipated sounding a triumphant call of victory, now I just wanted to go home to the arms of my wife. Wendy compassionately suggested I do just that.

We all knew the news of this verdict would not be an encouragement to the marchers.

It seemed appropriate that Willie and I sound our shofars over the hotel before the marchers and celebrants arrived. We walked the short distance to the corner opposite the Corinthian. A dozen policemen were assembled outside, and a security camera had been mounted above the entrance to monitor the "Protestors."

After praying and sounding our shofars, Willie began to notice symbolism in the ornamental concrete adorning the old hotel—scepters and royal seals, and higher up, a scaly serpent encircling the entire structure.

But above it all, just below the roof line, were ornamental lion heads.

We immediately understood in these symbols that the "The Lion of Judah" was above the serpent and always would be, as the Bible says. We shouted joyfully.

I recounted the lion heads from that morning's walk, and thanked God for yet another encouragement.

Moments later, two elderly homeless men, one in a wheelchair and one pushing, hurried toward us. The man sitting in the wheelchair, smiling joyfully, shook our hands, and said, "We came at the sound of the shofars!"

They were in a hurry and did not stop. And all the while, the man pushing kept shouting excitedly, "Sound of Judah! Sound of Judah!"

After another moment, an elderly Jewish man and his wife approached. They were well dressed, and he introduced himself as a long-time Houston Judge. He said they'd been excited to hear shofars, and that he'd never seen shofars on this corner before.

As they departed, he added that they were just coming from a wedding he had performed.

Having studied Jewish heritage and customs, we began to understand what we'd just witnessed:

- The King of Judah.
- The Sound of Judah.
- A Jewish Wedding.

Horn of Samuel

These related to the Biblical pattern seen in Jewish wedding custom. There, a much anticipated bridegroom arrives at a time no one knows, and is announced by the sounding of the shofar.

The Corinthian Hotel was less than two blocks from the courthouse. Just below the roof line, lion heads are positioned above a scaly serpent that wraps around the entire building.

The lion heads represented Jesus, or 'Yeshua', the Lion King of Judah. Biblically, He is the Bridegroom, and His believers are the bride. The book of Revelation is the "unveiling of the bride" when the church is "revealed" to the Bridegroom.

Heaven's Trumpet Call of Liberty

Revelation also describes the bride preparing by cleansing herself. And the bride [church] today is covered by the crimson stain of abortion. Cleansing involves remorse and repentance, which is reflected in all of those hurt by abortion, realizing that they have been deceived, telling God they are sorry, and receiving His forgiveness. Many of the counselors now ministering on the sidewalks of abortion clinics have this testimony.

In the ballroom of this old hotel, Parenthood would soon be celebrating the opening of its largest abortion clinic in the United States. Our shofars had just provided a warning of the approach of the Bridegroom.

We left before the protestors arrived. I watched the march that night on the local TV News. [The Lady] was interviewed—she'd led this charge against the giant.

My spirit would need more solace, and it arrived the next morning. I'd been invited to sound the shofar on May 1st, over a Jewish celebration known as "The Day of the Child." It is celebrated about two thirds of the way between the Feast Days of Passover and Pentecost.

The trial had ended just the day before, between these particular Feast Days. That morning, Lloyd, Quincey, and I gathered with family and friends at a city park. We prepared by praying and donning our Tallits.

We first sounded in sequence, individually, four times, turning in formation to face each point of the compass. We then stood back-to-back, and lifted our shofars straight up, sounding in unison into heaven.

Next, we sounded softly over a lady named Darlene, as she danced and sang of her love for Jesus.

I was then called to the front of the gathering, alone. They asked that the battle cry, or "Teruah," be sounded over the children.

They had no idea of the events of the previous day. But looking out over a sea of children's smiles, I sounded a bold "Teruah", proclaiming God's Love and protection over His children.

Tau-Tau-Tau-Tau-Tau-Tau-Tau-Tau-Tau!

Tau-Tau-Tau-Tau-Tau-Tau-Tau-Tau-Tau!

Tau-Tau-Tau-Tau-Tau-Tau-Tau-Tau-Tau!

I believed God was telling me He has always sounded His trumpet call of victory over every child given to abortion, and that they are all just fine—they are all safe, and over-shaded by His great love.

God had freed me from the dark prison of regret, and put me in a place of honor to sound the trumpet call of His Love for children. Unbelievable.

And He is faithful to do that for every broken heart surrendered to Him.

It is like being in a dark, hopeless prison—but you are entitled to make one call. The jailers cannot stop you.

You have a direct line to the heavenly Defender that has never lost a case. And He waits patiently to receive your call, and to set you free.

God sounded forth the ultimate, victorious trumpet call with the death and resurrection of His own dear Son. He knows what it is to give up a child. He knows your pain, personally.

God has left it up to you. You have the choice of remaining in a dark prison, or calling out to a Father God who knows you and loves you in spite of everything. Won't you make that call now? It's free. Oh, so free.

"Father God, help me to know Your love. I believe Your Son, Jesus, died on the cross at Calvary for my sins, and rose again. I surrender all my sins to You. Please heal my broken heart, and fill it with the Love of heaven."

PS: THE PROOF

During the first day of the trial, three prosecution witnesses used the color of my shirt to identify me. They were the only witnesses to use the color of my shirt.

As the Court records show, one witness said, "Lavender," and two said, "Purple."

The shirt I was wearing was light blue. It was a Van Huesen dress shirt as blue as the morning sky. On the back cover, there's a picture of me in front of the court building with Mary and Susan, wearing this same shirt.

In the Bible, purple symbolizes royalty. And Jesus is referred to as the "King of kings." And on the cross, Jesus had a sign hung above His head that said, "The King of the Jews." It appears these witnesses saw the covering of my heavenly Defender during the trial.

As each witness mentioned the color of my shirt, I would turn to my Armor Bearer and whisper, "the color of the King!" Each time, he would smile and nod.

To me, this was a miracle. But for the skeptic in all of us, there is some further evidence.

At the start of the trial, the prosecutor had invoked "The Rule." This meant that witnesses were not allowed to hear the testimony of other witnesses, and therefore, each witness could only be in the courtroom during their own testimony. They could not have heard or been influenced by the testimony of others.

The witnesses were also instructed not to discuss their testimony outside the courtroom. In any event, a minor detail like the color of a shirt would probably not have come up even if they did talk. So the possibility that the witnesses were influenced by earlier witnesses may be ruled out.

A second possibility might be that the lighting in the courtroom made my shirt appear purple. But it so happened that one of the "Pro-Life" attendees, Susan, was so impressed by this phenomenon, that she wanted to do an experiment.

Susan has an analytical mind, and after the trial, asked if I would help her. We'd go back to the courtroom and ask volunteers, unfamiliar with the events, to sit in the witness stand, while I sat at the defense table, wearing the same blue shirt and Tallit I'd worn at trial. The volunteers would then be asked to identify the color of my shirt.

I contacted the Court to ask permission, and to coordinate an acceptable time. The Judge happened to be on vacation the week we wanted to conduct our experiment, but a Clerk said we could come by and see if it didn't work out.

Susan and I met outside the courtroom just before lunch on Tuesday, June 29th, anticipating the Court would be empty at that time. I was wearing the same clothing I'd worn that day, including my Tallit.

Peeking through the blinds in the back windows we could see there was no Judge on the bench, but that Court business was still being conducted. At the prosecutor's table, Joshua and Stacey were working.

As we waited in the hallway, Stacey walked out and saw us. I waved and smiled, but she frowned and passed by to use her cell phone. After she returned to the courtroom, Joshua came out. He was unshaven and roughly dressed; not like the polished attorney I'd observed at trial.

He said accusingly, "Oh, still not Jewish, and still wearing the Tallit." I responded, "You are loved, Joshua."

Ignoring me, he demanded to know why we were there. As Susan tried to explain, he became upset when he concluded that we wanted to find some fault with the trial testimony.

When I tried to assure him that was not the case, he leaned close to Susan and said, "I don't want to communicate with him at all." He then continued a heated cross examination, without allowing answers to his questions.

At this point we were crowded together in a small alcove outside one of the doors into the courtroom. I wanted to leave and go in, but Joshua was in the way.

As Susan explained that we wanted to do an "experiment," he laughed, and asked, "Are you a scientist now?"

She replied, "I have a degree in geology...." But he cut her off and demanded to know the exact nature of the experiment.

When Susan explained that we wanted a witness to identify the color of my shirt, he looked at my shirt, and angrily shouted, "IT'S BLUE!"

That was all I could take. I said, "Come on Susan, we're going in," and led the way past him and into the courtroom.

As we attempted to take seats in the gallery pews, Joshua entered behind us and proceeded to the center of the Courtroom. He waved an arm in the air and announced, "Mr. Allen is here to further distort the truth!"

Everyone in the Courtroom, Defendants, clerks, and Bailiffs alike, stared in silent amazement as he made various charges. I responded, "Joshua, you are truly loved. You are a special child to your Father God."

When it was clear he wasn't going to allow us to sit, I crossed over to the Court Clerk, and as is customary, stood outside the gate waiting to be motioned through to communicate with the Clerk.

Still Joshua continued, and I responded again, "You are a special man Joshua, and deeply loved."

With that, he came near and leaned over the clerk's table. Turning his head to look at me, he whispered something that only I could hear. And while I can't share that here, it told me of Joshua's hurting heart.

He then straightened up, and pointed to the chair at the defense table, and said firmly, "Sit Down!"

I stood frozen, not wanting to submit.

Still pointing at the chair and glaring at me, he repeated the demand by shouting, "SIT DOWN!"

I entered through the gate, and sat down in the chair.

Waving his arm, he commanded Susan, "Take the witness stand!" She entered the gate on the other side of the courtroom, climbed the steps, and sat down.

He then demanded to know if we were satisfied, and, without waiting for an answer, indicated that we should leave.

Ignoring him, I returned to my place outside the gate, and continued waiting for the Clerk. At this point Joshua and Stacey gathered their files and left.

When the Clerk at last called me forward, I passed through the gate and stood before her. She looked at me with a blank, quizzical expression, as though wondering what planet I was from.

I groped for words, but could only say, "Please extend my regards to the Judge when he returns."

As we took an empty elevator to the first floor, and walked out to the sidewalk, I felt disheartened that Joshua had ruined our experiment.

Suddenly, I stopped and smiled.

"Susan!" I exclaimed, "Joshua said it was blue! The Prosecutor was our witness!"

PPS: A FINAL BLESSING

Sunday morning following the trial, I was still feeling a sense of shock, wondering, "How could this deceitful giant still be standing?"

I was cooking pancakes on a griddle as my three boys were beginning to stir. Nine year old Daniel walked in sleepily to watch.

Musically gifted, he'd been learning "The Battle Hymn of the Republic." He'd found it programmed on his electric keyboard, but I'd been oblivious to his efforts.

Daniel asked, "Dad, what does that verse mean, the one about, "the Hero born of woman who crushes the serpent with His heel?'"

Remembering the serpent on the Corinthian Hotel, I immediately stopped, and went to the computer to find the lyrics to the hymn. I learned that the hymn was written during the Civil War, and was about the tyranny of slavery. I'd mentioned that war on the steps of City Hall a week earlier, and again at the trial.

The words Daniel was asking about were, "Let the Hero born of woman crush the serpent with His heel." I explained to him that this refers to Jesus and His bride [the church] stepping on Satan's head, (Genesis 3:15, Romans 16:20).

Horn of Samuel

I then began singing the vaguely familiar verses and the words began to come more boldly. Another verse caught my attention and it filled the house as I sang:

> "He has sounded forth the trumpet that shall never call retreat,
> He is sifting out the hearts of men before His judgment seat,
> O be swift my soul to answer Him! Be jubilant my feet!
> Our God is marching on.
>
> Glory, glory, hallelujah!
> Glory, glory, hallelujah!
> Glory, glory, hallelujah!
> Our God is marching on."

Sounding shofars at a Praise and Worship gathering in North Houston are (l to r) Sean Jones, David Allen, Douglas Flores, and Michael Mireles.